Barragem
de Odeleite

Barragem
de Beliche

Serra de Alcária do Cume

E

Guadiana

Castro
Marim

Vila Real
de Santo António

São Brás
de Alportel

E01

Cacela
Velha

A22

Golfo   de   Cádiz

Milreu

Serra de Monte Figo

Tavira

IP1

Estói

Ilha de Tavira

ro:
dade Velha

Olhão

Ilha da Armona

Parque
Natural da Ria
Formosa

TWINPACK
Algarve

SALLY ROY

If you have any comments
or suggestions for this guide
you can contact the editor at
Twinpacks@theAA.com

AA Publishing
Find out more about AA Publishing and the wide
range of services the AA provides by visiting our
website at theAA.com/bookshop

How to Use This Book

KEY TO SYMBOLS

✚ Map reference

✉ Address

☎ Telephone number

🕐 Opening/closing times

🍴 Restaurant or café

🚆 Nearest rail station

🚌 Nearest bus route

⛴ Nearest ferry or riverboat route

♿ Facilities for visitors with disabilities

❓ Other practical information

▷ Further information

ℹ Tourist information

✋ Admission charges:
Expensive (over €8),
Moderate (€3–€8), and
Inexpensive (under €3)

★ Major Sight   ★ Minor Sight

👣 Walks   🚌 Drives

🎁 Shops

🎵 Entertainment and Activities

🍴 Restaurants

This guide is divided into four sections

• Essential Algarve: An introduction to the region and tips on making the most of your stay.
• Algarve by Area: We've broken the region into four areas, and recommended the best sights, shops, activities, restaurants, entertainment and nightlife venues in each one. Suggested walks and drives help you to explore.
• Where to Stay: The best hotels, whether you're looking for luxury, budget or something in between.
• Need to Know: The info you need to make your trip run smoothly, including getting about by public transport, weather tips, emergency phone numbers and useful websites.

Navigation In the Algarve by Area chapter, we've given each area its own colour, which is also used on the locator maps throughout the book and the map on the inside front cover.

Maps The fold-out map accompanying this book is a comprehensive map of the Algarve. The grid on this fold-out map is the same as the grid on the locator maps within the book. The grid references to these maps are shown with capital letters, for example A1. The grid references to the town plan are shown with lower-case letters, for example a1.

Contents

CONTENTS

Introducing the Algarve

Sun. Sand. Sea. Eight people out of ten look for this trio of must-haves when planning a holiday, which is precisely why, in less than 50 years, the Algarve has been transformed from a remote, poor, coastal region to an international, year-round playground.

What do you need in a holiday playground? Sun, sand and sea obviously, but it's the add-ons that the Algarve delivers so well. Along this 135-km stretch (84 miles) of coast and hinterland there's scenery to suit all tastes; lagoons, rivers, dunes, coves and dramatic cliffs, mountains, woods and rich farmland, historic towns and booming resorts. Factor in an efficient infrastructure and a long tradition of hospitality, and it's easy to understand the pride the Portuguese take in the Algarve.

In the 1960s, when it all started, Portugal was determined not to make the same mistakes as Spain. Early building in what were then still fishing villages was restrained, with the emphasis on quality. It couldn't last, and the Algarve today has plenty of high-rise developments, while the infamous N125, the main through route, is fringed in parts with dreary commercial buildings.

But turn off down to the coast, and all this is behind you. Here are the glorious beaches, the golf courses, the hotels, restaurants and bars. The diverse resorts of the Algarve provide something for every taste and pocket.

Tourism has brought incalculable changes to local lives. Set aside the huge economic benefits, leading to better health, education and opportunities, and what emerges? Some Portuguese would say problems—depopulation of the interior, decline in agriculture and potential water problems due to excessive irrigation. But ask an old fisherman what he thinks of his grandchildren attending university, and you'll hear nothing but enthusiasm for today's Algarve. Ask any visitor, too, what brings them back year after year, and the answer will echo what initially wrought the changes—the sun, the sea, the way of life and the hospitality and kindness of the people.

Facts + Figures

- Size: the Algarve is 155km (96 miles) long and 50km (31 miles) wide
- Population: 400,000
- Golf Courses: 35
- Average days of sunshine per year: 300

BEACHES FOR ALL SEASONS

The Algarve offers huge stretches of sand, coves and cliffs and most of the beaches have been awarded the EU Blue Flag for water quality and cleanliness. Importantly, in summer even remote beaches have a lifeguard as many of them slope precipitously and have dangerous crosscurrents.

SARDINHAS

Nothing better conjures up the atmosphere of an Algarve holiday than the scent of grilled sardines. This little fish, properly in season during the summer, but now eaten all year, is in fact several different fish of the herring/mackerel variety; sardine is the generic term for a certain size. Eat them hot off the grill, with a squeeze of lemon and plenty of salt.

SNOW IN THE ALGARVE

Legend tells of the marriage of a Moorish king to a beautiful Scandinavian princess. He brought her to Silves, plied her with gifts and loved her deeply, but she was unhappy; she missed the northern snows. So the king planted thousands of almond trees and, for a few short weeks in spring, she saw the hillsides white, with the 'Algarvian snow'.

A Short Stay in the Algarve

DAY 1: FARO

Morning Start your day with a leisurely exploration of the **Cidade Velha** (▷ 74), taking in the **Sé**. Climb the bell tower for some sparkling views over the lagoon and the town before walking on to learn more about Faro's history at the **Museu Municipal de Faro** (▷ 75), where, after tracing the town's fascinating Roman past, you can soak up the tranquillity of the beautiful cloisters of this old convent. Time for a break and you can walk down to the harbourside and enjoy coffee at the terrace bar next to the Jardim Manuel Bivar, before passing an hour or so mingling with local shoppers in Faro's pedestrian-only central core just across the road from the Jardim.

Lunch Seek out a table at **Coffee Aliança** (▷ 87) and enjoy a light lunch at one of Portugal's oldest coffee houses.

Afternoon Enjoy **a stroll** (▷ 84) round the town, spending a quiet moment in one of Faro's churches, and marvelling at the wealth of decoration. To learn more about the local way of life, spend a half-hour or so in the **Museu Regional do Algarve** (▷ 84), before heading down to the harbour to enjoy a drink or to learn about the sea at **Centro Ciência Viva** (▷ 86), one of Faro's most child-friendly attractions.

Dinner Eat dinner at **A Taska** (▷ 87) and sample a real Algarve specialty such as bean rice with fish or fried squid in one of the two cosy dining rooms.

Evening Finish your day by either heading out to the Teatro Municipal das Figuras de Faro to catch a performance, or by indulging in some late-night retail therapy at the **Forum Algarve** (▷ 85).

DAY 2: LAGOS

Morning The best introduction to Lagos (▷ 26) is to simply walk the streets, so kick off by strolling downhill beside the wonderful old town walls from the **Forte da Ponte da Bandeira**. Take in the **Praça Infante Dom Henrique** and the old **slave market** before relaxing for morning coffee at one of the square's café terraces. After this, head up to the **Museu Municipal**, where you can spend a fascinating hour or so examining the quirky exhibits—don't miss the model of typical Algarve buildings and activities, or the Roman amphora excavated along the coast at **Boca da Rio** (▷ 38).

Lunch Choose one of the many restaurants on or around **Praça Luís de Camões** (▷ 27) or head for **O Artista** (▷ 44) where you can enjoy anything from a simple snack to a three-course lunch.

Afternoon Head down to the waterfront for an afternoon by the sea. The simplest option is to relax on the sands of the town beach below the fortress, or you could cross the River Bensafrim and make for the sands of **Meia Praia** (▷ 29). **Boat trips** (▷ 41) to other beaches leave regularly from near the marina—opt for one that takes in the extraordinary rock formations at **Ponte da Piedade** (▷ 28), and offers a chance for a swim on the way back.

Dinner After an aperitif in the town, climb the stairs to **Estrela do Mar** (▷ 43), where you can dine on fish while taking in the views from the top of the market building.

Evening Head for **Stevie Ray's** (▷ 41), for live jazz and other sounds, some great mixed drinks and a lively atmosphere.

Top 25

►►►

Albufeira ▷ 70 The Algarve's busiest resort still has some of the elements that first drew the tourists.

Alte ▷ 72 Sparkling white, picturesque hill village in the heart of the fertile inland Barrocal.

Cabo de São Vicente ▷ 24 Headland where the west coast of Europe turns east to the Mediterranean.

West Coast Beaches ▷ 34 Peace, quiet, cliffs, beaches and surfing waves are found in the Costa Vicentina Natural Park.

Water Parks ▷ 58 Summertime sees slides and rides in operation at the Algarve's water parks.

Vila Real de Santo António ▷ 100 An architecturally homogenous town with a grid plan of 18th-century streets.

Vilamoura ▷ 81 A purpose-built resort with a stylish marina, slick hotels and manicured golf courses.

Tavira ▷ 98 Lovely 18th- and 19th-century buildings, churches and a ruined Moorish castle line the streets of this elegant town.

Silves ▷ 56 The Moorish capital is dominated by a superb castle and beautiful Gothic cathedral.

Sagres: Fortaleza de Sagres ▷ 32 Henry the Navigator's fortress where ships were once designed.

Sagres ▷ 30 A township in the far west that's surrounded by towering cliffs.

Rio Guadiana ▷ 96 A navigable river forms the Algarve border between Spain and Portugal.

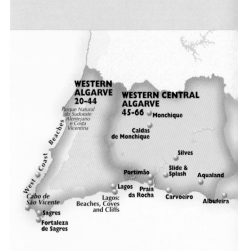

WESTERN ALGARVE 20–44
Parque Natural do Sudoeste Alentejano e Costa Vicentina

WESTERN CENTRAL ALGARVE 45–66

Monchique

Caldas de Monchique

West Coast Beaches

Silves

Portimão
Slide & Splash
Aqualand

Lagos
Praia da Rocha
Carvoeiro
Albufeira

Cabo de São Vicente
Lagos: Beaches, Coves and Cliffs

Sagres
Fortaleza de Sagres

These pages are a quick guide to the Top 25, which are described in more detail later. Here they are listed alphabetically, and the tinted background shows which area they are in.

Caldas de Monchique and Monchique ▷ 48
A delightful spa village and nearby hill town.

Carvoeiro and Around ▷ 50 A former fishing village with a beautiful coastline and great beaches.

Estói ▷ 73 Quite simply, the most beautiful baroque palace in the Algarve, with enchanting gardens.

Faro: Cidade Velha ▷ 74 A walled city, above a harbour, that's crammed with historic buildings.

Igreja Capela de São Lourenço dos Matos ▷ 76 The Algarve's most beautiful church.

Lagos: Beaches, Coves and Cliffs ▷ 28 Sweeping sands, coves and rock formations surround the town of Lagos.

Lagos Town ▷ 26 An historic town that's retained its medieval walls, cobbled streets and fine buildings.

Loulé ▷ 78 This inland town has its roots in Moorish times.

Olhão ▷ 92 Superbly workaday fishing port where the accent is on fish.

Paderne ▷ 80 This splendid castle, its outer walls intact, highlights the Algarve's Moorish legacy.

Parque Natural da Ria Formosa ▷ 94 A park that's home to superb bird and marine life.

Praia de Rocha ▷ 54 The Algarve's oldest resort with a south-facing beach and buzzing nightlife.

Portimão ▷ 52 Bustling town and river port that's famous for its riverside sardine restaurants.

Map labels:
Parque Natural do Vale do Guardiana
EASTERN ALGARVE 89–106 (E)
Guadiana
EASTERN CENTRAL ALGARVE 67–88
Paderne
Loulé
Vilamoura
Estói
Igreja Capela de São Lourenço dos Matos
Faro: Cidade Velha
Olhão
Tavira
Vila Real de Santo António
Parque Natural da Ria Formosa

◀ ◀ ◀

Out and About

The fabulous beaches, year-round mild temperatures and hot summer sun were the impetus for tourism development in the Algarve, so it's hardly surprising that most visitors spend all day, every day, outside. Many are content to lie by the pool or on the beach day after day, but there's a lot more than that to the Algarve, and a bit of variety will spice up your holiday.

Beaches

The main draw is the beaches, which, considering the size of the Algarve, vary tremendously. As a general rule, the further west you get, the higher the cliffs and the wilder the sea, so if you like sheltered, warm waters and long smooth beaches, you'll enjoy the coast east of Faro. The central Algarve is a mix of every element, with some huge, sandy beaches and dozens of beguiling coves and bays. These charms pull the crowds, and you can expect this stretch to be more developed and crowded than elsewhere. Head west to escape, where you'll find a wild and protected coast, where there's little development and superb beaches, but a year-round wind and dangerous Atlantic swells just offshore.

Watery Pleasures

The bigger resorts all have a great range of differing water sports—everything from a gentle boat trip chugging along the base of the cliffs to admire the spectacular rock formations for

GOLFING PACKAGES

If you just turn up at the golf courses you can expect to pay substantial green fees everywhere and sky-high ones at the championship courses. Factor in the hassle of booking a tee time and it's easy to see why golf packages are big business in the Algarve. Specialist companies (such as www.costalessgolf.com) arrange all-in holidays that include flights, accommodation, transport to and from a selection of courses, green fees, and those other little extras, leaving you free to simply enjoy the golf.

From top: Bright parasols line the beach; playing ball on the sand; water skiing; fishing off a rock stack

which the Algarve is famous, to the thrills of jet boats and water-skiing, scuba diving and surfing some of the best breaks in Europe. With the growing interest in the environment, there's an increasing range of ecologically-friendly maritime activities, so, while big-game fishing still has its fans, other holidaymakers prefer to go whale and dolphin watching—you can even swim with dolphins in the Algarve.

Golf

With 35 golf courses and more under construction, the Algarve is a top destination for players all year. The courses range from tough 18-hole championship layouts to 9-holers that welcome novice golfers. The courses are beautiful, with sweeps of brilliant green fairway, shade trees and bunkers and water hazards that add to the visual attraction of the course as much as they challenge the golfer. Virtually all the courses have professionals to hand and will hire out equipment, trolleys and golf buggies.

What Else…?

For exercise fans, resort hotels offer everything from well-equipped gyms and pools to tennis courts, squash and bowling. Some run fitness programmes, either tailor-made for the guest or classes of aerobics, step-dancing, Pilates, Tai Chi and yoga, and will advise on diet and spa treatments. Head away from the coast to enjoy riding through the hills, or get walking through untouched countryside that's a long way in spirit from the packed beaches.

From top: Playing golf at Vale do Lobo; golf with a sea view; Hotel Luz Bay; the pool at Hotel Alvor Praia

RESORT HOTELS

Resort hotels are an excellent bet for families with children past the toddler stage. They all have great sports facilities in the shape of several pools, tennis courts, huge grounds, private beaches, often with water sports laid on, and access to dozens of other options which they can arrange for you. Most sports at such hotels are included in the price, making them a good option if you've got teenagers who want a constant stream of entertainment.

Shopping

It has to be said that shopping in the Algarve is not the number one leisure activity, and you may be quite content never to set foot in a shop during your stay. But, when the beach palls, there's plenty on offer, from trawling the malls to browsing in the great range of local stores or picking up culinary specialties in the markets.

Artesanato

Artesanato shops specialize in Portuguese artisan products, ranging from the traditional Roman-designed chairs made at Monchique, through basketry, cork products and rugs to textiles, hand-knitted sweaters and a vast range of ceramics and pottery. You'll find pottery outlets everywhere, selling hand-painted plates, bowls and tableware—it's worth visiting several and taking your time to track down what really appeals. Other craft shops are found in most resorts, though the market town of Loulé, with its long tradition of handicrafts, is the best bet.

Markets

All towns of any size have a daily market, ideal for picking up a picnic or seeking out food products to take home; look out for local cheese, ham and sausage, honey from the hills, olives and dried fruit, spices and herbs and delicious almond-based biscuits and confectionary. Weekly markets, called gypsy markets, operate in each town and sell leather goods and shoes, clothes, table and bed linen and CDs, cheap jewellery and beach wear.

THE MALLS

The Algarve has three major shopping malls, the Forum Algarve, on the western outskirts of Faro, the Guia Algarve Shopping Centre near Albufeira, and Ria Shopping at Olhão. They have the full range of international chain stores, food courts and cinemas, and each runs buses from and to the surrounding resorts. There are smaller shopping centres at Albufeira, Faro, Loulé, Portimão and Silves.

Local goods for sale include pretty, hand-woven rugs, wooden stools, gourds and cockerel pottery

Algarve by Night

After a day on the beach, start your evening with a relaxing drink at a terrace bar, either choosing a spot overlooking the sea as the sun sets, or grabbing a table where you can watch the world go by. After dinner, enjoy a stroll and a late-night drink, hit the town by heading for a club or casino, or take in a bit of culture.

Music, Dance and Film
Many big hotels will have nightly entertainment with music and dancing, and you'll find bars with live music everywhere in the Algarve. For more serious cultural pleasures, time your trip to coincide with one of the region's big shindigs, such as the International Music Festival, which stages concerts and ballet from June to August, the 'Allgarve' Festival, with big international acts, or the July International Jazz Festival in Loulé. All films in Portugal are shown in their original language, so you can catch the blockbusters at cinemas throughout the area.

Clubbing till Late, Late, Late
The big resorts are home to the flashiest clubs, where you can hit the dance floor from around midnight through to dawn, though summer sees something for night birds just about everywhere. There's a wide choice of music at these venues, so all ages can strut their stuff. For something quieter in the wee small hours, head for a casino, where you'll find the full range of table games and myriad machines; the casinos also stage floor shows and often disco nights.

The Algarve offers varied nightlife from drinking cocktails by the sea to live music, casinos and clubs

FADO
You may have the chance to hear *fado*, Portugal's soul music, a unique performance art, where each song expresses the sadness that lies at the root of even the greatest human happiness; the yearning for love, for home, for the past. It's performed by a singer and two musicians who accompany the *fadista* on the 12-stringed *quitarra portuguesa* and a Spanish guitar.

Eating Out

Eating out in the Algarve is a real pleasure. There are restaurants, bars and cafés to suit every taste, with culinary styles and chefs from all over the world, and an emphasis on fresh local produce from the land and fish from the sea.

Lunch and Dinner

Lunch *(almoço)* is still the main meal for the locals, a three-course blow-out that traditionally includes soup, a hefty main course and pudding. It's worth checking out the set meal *(ementa turistica)*, comprising three courses and a drink, and the *prato do dia*, the daily special, which will often be a local specialty. Portions are huge, and include potatoes and/or rice and vegetables. Dinner *(jantar)* follows the same pattern. As well as restaurants, the Algarve offers *tascas* (taverns), *churrascarias* (specializing in grilled meat and fish) and *marisquerias*, where the accent is firmly on fish and seafood. Except at very grand establishments, there's no need to dress up.

Watching the Budget

It's perfectly possible to eat well and cheaply in the Algarve. Choose the *ementa turistica*, and take advantage of the plentiful sardines. Other good buys include pizza, pasta and the all-inclusive meals served by many foreign-owned bars and restaurants. Lunchtime and early-evening menus are also often cheaper. Top up with fruit from the market, *galao* (milky coffee) and *pastelaria* (cakes and pastries) at a local café and enjoy the taste of the Algarve.

RESERVATIONS

It's not necessary to book at typically Portuguese restaurants, unless they are pretty up-market; if there's no table, simply wait at the bar for one to become available, or come back later. Booking is advised at upper-range restaurants, particularly for groups of four or more and at weekends. If there's somewhere you really want to eat, check out whether booking is necessary.

From top: Grilling sardines at Portimão; a restaurant with ocean views; marzipan delicacies; tasty seafood

Restaurants by Cuisine

There are restaurants to suit all tastes in the Algarve, with the accent on locally sourced and produced food. On this page they are listed by cuisine. For a more detailed description of each restaurant, see Algarve by Area.

ALGARVIAN

A Taska (▷ 87)
Adega Nortenha (▷ 87)
Afonso III (▷ 87)
Jardim das Oliveiras (▷ 66)
O Soeiro (▷ 106)
Paraíso do Montanha (▷ 66)

GRILLS

Adega do Papagaio (▷ 43)
Arenilha (▷ 106)
Cervejaria Praia da Rocha (▷ 66)
O Coração da Cidade (▷ 106)

INTERNATIONAL

A Vaca (▷ 43)
Boia Bar (▷ 43)

Fortaleza da Luz (▷ 43)
Malwa (▷ 106)
Vila Velha (▷ 44)
Willies (▷ 88)

ITALIAN

Fuzio's (▷ 88)
La Mona Lisa (▷ 66)

MEDITERRANEAN

Aquasul (▷ 106)
Izzy's Restaurant and Beach Bar (▷ 88)
Memmo Baleeira Sagres (▷ 44)

PORTUGUESE

Beach Bar (▷ 43)
Churrasqueira a Tenazinha (▷ 87)

Coffee Aliança (▷ 87)
Mar á Vista (▷ 44)
O Artista (▷ 44)
O Rei dos Frangos (▷ 88)
O Zuco (▷ 88)

SEAFOOD/FISH

A Ruina (▷ 87)
A Tasca (▷ 43)
Ababuja (▷ 65)
Bica Velha (▷ 87)
Casa Velha (▷ 65)
Estrela do Mar (▷ 43)
Mira Mar (▷ 44)
Nortada (▷ 44)
Quatro Aguas (▷ 106)
Sueste (▷ 66)
U Venâncio (▷ 66)

If You Like...

However you'd like to spend your time in the Algarve, these ideas should help you tailor your perfect visit. Each suggestion has a fuller write-up elsewhere in the book.

A TOUCH OF RETAIL THERAPY

Head for one of the Algarve's malls (▷ 12), and take your pick of the international chain stores.
Don't miss browsing in one of the region's pottery outlets; Porches (▷ 63) is the best place with the widest choice.
Hit Loulé Saturday market (▷ 85) and track down some specialty food souvenirs.

Pottery urns for sale at Porches (above)

A TASTE OF THE SEA

Enjoy fish and seafood at A Tasca in Sagres (▷ 43), where you can eat above the harbour where your fish was landed.
Watch the evening darken as you eat fish on the terrace of A Ruina (▷ 87), overlooking Albufeira beach.
Munch sardines, cooked on the outside grill, at Ababuja (▷ 65), by the harbour at Alvor.

Sunset at Fisherman's Beach, Albufeira (above)

THE BEST OF PORTUGUESE CUISINE

Sample the best of mountain cooking at Jardim das Oliveiras (▷ 66), high in the Serra de Monchique.
Join the locals to eat some of the best *frango piri-piri* (hot and spicy chicken) you've ever sampled at Churrasqueria a Tenazinha (▷ 87).
Enjoy up-country food and river fish at O Soeiro (▷ 106), overlooking the River Guadiana.

Freshly caught sardines being cooked on a barbecue (above). The coastal town Burgau (below)

HOTELS AWAY FROM THE CROWDS

Check in at Casa Grande (▷ 109) in Burgau, an old-fashioned guest house in an old-fashioned village.
Breathe the mountain air at the Estalegem Abrigo da Montanha (▷ 109), a mountain inn on the high slopes of Foia.
Spend a few days at Pensão Residencial Cantinho da Ria Formosa (▷ 111), a country house inn set in green fields not far from the sea.

*ncing
*e night
*ay (right).
*oying a
*nd of golf
elow)

STAYING UP LATE

Enjoy a floor show, hit the dance floor or have a serious flutter at the Casino Vilamoura (▷ 86).

Mingle with the Algarve's super-cool as you strut your stuff at Kadoc (▷ 86).

Dance till dawn to the sounds of guest DJs at Albufeira's famous Kiss club (▷ 86).

THE OUTDOOR LIFE

Play a round of golf at Vale do Lobo, Quinta do Lago or Vilamoura (▷ 86) and experience challenging golf on some of Europe's loveliest courses.

Brush up your racket skills on one of the courts at Carvoeiro Clube de Ténis (▷ 64).

Discover the ocean on a scuba dive with the Divers Cove team (▷ 64).

Mount up to explore the western Algarve on horseback from the Centro Hipico Quinta do Paraíso Alto (▷ 41).

VALUE FOR MONEY

Take a walk through Faro Old Town (▷ 74) to see the best of vernacular architecture and soak up the atmosphere.

Tuck into a great value plate of chicken piri-piri at O Rei dos Frangos (▷ 88) in Albufeira.

*Faro Old Town (above).
Pamper yourself with a
spa treatment (below)*

Spend a day in the sun and sea on any beach, anywhere.

Take the ferry at Tavira (▷ 98) and head for the Ilha de Tavira—14km (9 miles) of beaches and sandy walking paths.

TREATING YOURSELF

Indulge in a day's pampering at the spa at Le Méridien Penina (▷ 112) near Alvor.

Book a table for dinner at Willie's (▷ 88) at Vilamoura for some culinary magic.

Try some thalassatherapy (sea water treatment) at Vilalara (▷ 112).

ESSENTIAL ALGARVE IF YOU LIKE...

FUN WITH THE KIDS

Let them loose at a waterpark (▷ 58) and watch them let off steam.

Get them up close and personal with the animals at Lagos Zoo (▷ 41).

Combine the fun of the fair and plenty of watery rides with dolphin and sea-lion shows at Zoomarine (▷ 86).

Sample the lighter side of science with the interactive exhibits at the Centro Ciência Viva attraction (▷ 86) in Faro.

A seal at Zoomarine, Albufeira (above)

THE SAND IN YOUR TOES

Head east or west from Vilamoura to the Praia da Marina and the Praia de Falésia (▷ 81).

Explore the coves and beaches west of Lagos (▷ 28).

Head up the wild west coast (▷ 34) to discover untouched sand and magnificent seas.

Take in the wildlife and beaches of the Parque Natural da Ria Formosa (▷ 94).

Parque Natural da Ria Formosa (above)

MESSING ABOUT IN BOATS

Cruise up the beautiful river valley of the Rio Guadiana with Riosul (▷ 96).

Step aboard a traditional river boat in Portimão and head upstream with Arade Mar (▷ 64) to explore Silves.

See the caves and grottoes, swim off the boat and enjoy a barbeque on the Santa Bernarda (▷ 64), a replica *caravela* based in Portimão.

Sail from Lagos on high-speed RIBs to go dolphin watching with Algarve Dolphins (▷ 41).

Enjoying a boat trip on the River Arade (above). Detail of an azulejo *at São Lourenço church (below)*

A LITTLE TOUCH OF CULTURE

Take in the eclectic collection at the Museu Municipal in Lagos (▷ 27).

See some of the best *azulejos* (painted tiles) in Portugal at the church of São Lourenço (▷ 76).

Trace the Algarve's past at the Roman villa at Milreu (▷ 82).

Check out the Museu Municipal in Faro (▷ 75); the exhibits trace 2,000 years of history.

Algarve by Area

WESTERN ALGARVE

WESTERN CENTRAL ALGARVE

EASTERN CENTRAL ALGARVE

EASTERN ALGARVE

Dramatic coastal scenery fringes the western Algarve, a largely unspoiled area running from just east of Lagos around Cabo de São Vicente to Aljezur. Relaxed resorts are strung along the coast while inland, agricultural countryside gradually rises to the hills of the Serra de Espinhaço.

Foz do Besteiro

346
Fonte Santa

Besteiro

Romeiras

IP1

Odeáxere

Sargaçal

I25

Marateca

Portelas

Lagos

*Baia de
Lagos*

*Ponte da
Piedade*

**Lagos:
Beaches, Coves
and Cliffs**

| 0 | | 5 km |
| 0 | | 3 miles |

D   E   F

Cabo de São Vicente

TOP 25

Stunning view from the headland (left); textiles for sale (right); the lighthouse (opposite)

THE BASICS

- ➕ A7
- ✉ Near Sagres
- 🍴 Foodstands near lighthouse
- ♿ None
- ❓ Nearby: Sagres

DID YOU KNOW?

● The tiny fortress you'll pass on your way to the Cape is Beliche, and the beach below is the site from which Henry the Navigator's prototype *caravels* were launched, far away from prying eyes that might want to copy their super-fast and revolutionary design.

TIP

● The wind blows hard even in high summer, so take an extra sweater with you.

Europe's south-westernmost point is a dramatic and soaring headland, pounded by powerful Atlantic surf, from where there are superb views up and down the coast of the western Algarve.

The End of the World Cabo de São Vicente is the most south-westerly point of mainland Europe, a dramatic headland rising 75m (246ft) above the sea. The Romans called it the *Promontorium Sacrum* (the Sacred Promontory) and the ancient mariners *O Fim do Mundo* (The End of the World). In early Christian times, legend tells that a ship bearing the bones of St. Vincent came here from Spain to escape the Moors, giving the saint's name to the cape. It's still a special place, its wild sea, constant wind and clarity of light giving it a unique atmosphere.

At the Cape On the headland stands Europe's most powerful lighthouse, the light from its 3,000-watt bulb visible 100km (62 miles) out to sea. Though not officially open to the public, out of season the lighthouse keeper will sometimes give tours of the complex, which was once a coastal fortress and includes the ruins of a 16th-century monastery. The sunsets here are often superb, particularly in rough weather, making it easy to see why the Romans believed the sun sank hissing into the water every night. Near the lighthouse you'll often see locals fishing off the cliffs with immensely long rods. The waters off the cape are among the richest in Portugal, attracting many marine bird species to fish in the green depths.

Lagos Town

TOP
25

HIGHLIGHTS

● Praça da República
● Slave market
● Praça Luís de Camões
● Praça Gil Eanes
● Museu Municipal
● Igreja de Santo António

TIP

● If you are driving, there's a good parking area on the waterfront opposite the marina.

Packed with history and atmosphere, Lagos, the biggest and most attractive town in the western Algarve, provides good eating, good shopping and a buzz lacking in the smaller western villages.

The Past Founded in Phoenician times, the old town of Lagos, encircled by medieval walls, lies on the River Bensafrim. Its heyday was the 15th century, when it was the departure port for the great voyages of discovery, and it was the Algarve capital from 1557 to 1755, when much of the town was destroyed by the earthquake.

Lagos Today Lagos waterfront, overlooking the River Bensafrim with its marina and fishing dock, is backed by lovely gardens and guarded at the sea end by the trim little 17th-century Forte da Ponte

Clockwise from left: A pretty shopping street; intricate gilded woodwork in the church of Santo António; an unusual outdoor sculpture; taking a stroll through Lagos marina

da Bandeira. Opposite here, the solid town walls run downhill to the Praça Infante Dom Henrique, with its fine bronze statue of the Navigator. Here too is the old custom house, whose small arcade was once the sad site of Europe's first slave market, operating from 1444. Slavery was abolished in Portugal in 1761. Behind here, on Rua General Alberto da Silveira, the Museu Municipal (Tue–Sun 9.30–12.30, 2–5; inexpensive) is a wonderfully idiosyncratic collection that includes the superb Igreja de Santo António (1710–20), a riot of baroque gilding. East from here you'll find shopping streets, pretty squares, and a huge range of bars, cafés and restaurants. The best of these are found round two pleasant mosaic-paved squares, the Praça Luis de Camões and the Praça Gil Eanes, from where it's a few steps back to the river and marina.

THE BASICS

- ➕ D6
- 🍴 Restaurants, bars and cafés
- 🚌 Buses to Portimão, Luz and Sagres
- 🚉 1km (0.6 miles) north-east of the middle of town
- ♿ Few
- 🚢 Tourist boats along coast
- ℹ Largo Marquês de Pombal, tel 282 764 111; Mon–Sat 10–6 (also Sun Jul–Aug)

Lagos: Beaches, Coves and Cliffs

TOP 25

Clustering around Lagos are some of the Algarve's most beautiful beaches and coves, where firm, clean sand, clear emerald water and wonderfully sculpted rock formations are the keynotes.

West of Lagos Named, unsurprisingly, the Costa d'Ouro (Gold Coast), the towering ochre cliffs west of Lagos, enfolding magnificent arcs of sand, are formed of soft limestone that has been eroded over the centuries into extraordinary caves, arches and pillars. The most famous examples of these are at Ponte da Piedade, which you can explore by boat from Lagos; or you can catch the sunset from the headland above the grotto. Heading west from town, the beaches of Batata, Estudantes and Pinhão are lovely coves enclosed within the cliffs and easily reachable on foot. Further west

The picturesque Praia Dona Ana beach (left); a tranquil bay (middle) and spectacular cliffs and rock formations (right) at Ponte da Piedade

lies Praia Dona Ana, whose glorious sands and superb swimming have ensured its iconic status as the quintessential beach, and beyond is Praia do Camilo, where a tunnel has been cut through the rock formation that separates the two halves of the beach. Further west again, the idyllic coves of Boneca and Balança, accessible only by boat, provide the ultimate castaway dream.

Meia Praia For a complete contrast, cross the River Bensafrim in Lagos and head for Meia Praia, a 4km (2.5-mile) stretch of the softest sand running to the Ria de Alvor. Meia has plenty of attractions in the shape of windsurfing, surfing, kitesurfing, sailing and water skiing, and there are bars, restaurants and toilets near the parking area to the west. If you wish to escape the crowds however, simply walk east through the dunes.

THE BASICS

✚ D6
🍴 Most beaches have bars and restaurants
♿ Meia Praia is classified as an accessible beach
🛳 Balança and Boneca beaches are only accessible by boat from Lagos
❓ None of the beaches to the west of Lagos have loungers or umbrellas for hire; bring your own as there is no shade

Sagres

● One of the most-prized catches at Sagres are *perceves*, goose barnacles, not caught in boats, but scraped, at risk to life and limb, off rocks that are only exposed at low tide. They look like pebbles and are unique to the Iberian peninsula. Cooked in sea water and eaten plain, they are the essence of the Atlantic.

Crouching on a windswept headland and ringed with superb beaches, the straggling town of Sagres, Europe's most south-westerly community, is an important fishing port with an end-of-the-world atmosphere.

The Town Bounded on the west by the Fortaleza (▷ 32) and to the east by the harbour, Sagres' houses are scattered over a wide area. From the west-end Praça da República, an appealing, sheltered square lined with cafés, Rua Comandante Matosa arrows straight east along the cliff tops to the Porto da Baleeira, Sagres' working harbour, where the trawlers come in and the catch is sold at the commercial fishmarket. Book here for a sunset trip to Cabo de São Vicente (▷ 24) or boat trips for dolphin and whale watching. Back

The sweeping golden sands of Praia de Mareta beach (left); fishing from a dramatic clifftop at Sagres (right)

up the hill, shops, bars and restaurants are all within an easy stroll. Further out are more shops and hotels, and the town's covered market.

The Beaches Sagres' beaches, with their often thundering surf, are a mecca for surfers, and several outfits run surfing courses and supply equipment. The prevailing west and south-westerly winds sweep in from the Atlantic year-round. The west-facing Tonel beach has some shelter and great views towards São Vicente, though Mareta, the first of the Algarve's south-facing beaches and right in town, is a better bet if you've got kids. Outside town, to the northwest, Beliche nestles in a wide and sheltered cove at the foot of spectacular cliffs, while to the east, Martinhal, backed by dunes, has smooth sand and is excellent for wind-surfing.

THE BASICS

🞦 A7
🍴 Restaurants, bars and cafés
🚌 Buses to Lagos
♿ None
🛈 Rua Comandante Matoso, tel 282 624 873; May–Sep Mon–Sat 9.30–1, 2–6; Oct–Apr Mon–Fri 9.30–12.30, 1.30–5.30

Sagres: Fortaleza de Sagres

HIGHLIGHTS

● Rosa dos Ventos
● Nossa Senhora da Graça
● View from the ramp and cliffs

TIPS

● Numerous coach parties arrive after 10am and leave around 5pm; you'll get more from your visit outside these times.
● Wrap up against the wind at the Fortaleza, even on hot, sunny days.

The name of Henry the Navigator, the father of Portuguese exploration, is inextricably linked with the Fortaleza at Sagres, a wonderfully evocative complex on an exposed headland at the far southwest of the Algarve.

Henry the Navigator In 1420, as the Portuguese sought trade routes to the east, Prince Henry the Navigator, third son of João I and Philippa of Lancaster, set up his School of Navigation at Sagres. He gathered around him Arab astronomers, cartographers from Spain and instrument makers whose astrolabes and sextants helped map the stars, making longer voyages into the unknown increasingly viable. Maps improved as the Portuguese pushed further and further south down the African coast, voyages only

Clockwise from left: The church of Nossa Senhora da Graça; visitors walking along the ramparts of the Fortaleza; the 16th-century church; a view across the water showing the imposing position of the Fortaleza on the clifftop

possible in the *caravel*, first designed at Sagres. Such ships eventually conquered the Atlantic.

The Fortaleza Henry's school occupied the headland, today a vast area bounded by massive walls and bastions, remodelled in the 18th century. Walk through here and you'll find yourself in a vast and windswept space, with a range of modern buildings ahead and the tiny 16th-century church of Nossa Senhora da Graça to the right. Climb the ramp to the right of the entrance complex for an overview of the area; below you and startlingly clear is the outline of the 39m-diameter (128ft) *Rosa dos Ventos*, a wind, or compass, rose. It was unearthed by accident in 1921 and certainly dates from Henry's time, but how it functioned is still a mystery. From here walk across to visit the tiny church.

THE BASICS

www.ippar.pt

🔲 A7

✉ Fortaleza de Sagres

☎ 282 620 140

🕐 Oct–Apr daily 10–6.30, May–Sep daily 10–8.30

⬚ Moderate

❓ Nearby: Sagres

West Coast Beaches

● You'll need a car to access many of the beaches; not all are signposted and access may be along a dirt track.
● If you're visiting remote beaches, be careful about the tides and strong currents.
● Take care on the cliff paths and descents to the beaches.
● There is no shade, so take an umbrella and a high factor sun cream; the wind can make temperatures and sun strength very deceptive.

For untouched, wild coastal scenery and unspoiled beaches, nowhere else in the Algarve can touch the remote west coast, saved from development by its inclusion within the Costa Vicentina Natural Park.

Beaches near Aljezur It's 5km (3 miles) or more from the little town of Aljezur (▷ 37) to a string of idyllic and remote beaches, most facing due west. North from Aljezur, a tarmac road leads to Armoreira, a beach backed by dunes and the estuary of the Aljezur River, which has wonderfully safe low-tide, sandy pools for children. Pick of the bunch are Monte Clérigo, which combines a huge stretch of sand with wonderful low-tide rock pools, some deep enough for swimming, and Arrifana, a curving beach sheltered by magnificent cliffs, which offers great bodysurfing. South of

The remote beaches on the Algarve's west coast offer beautiful, unspoiled scenery

here, Figueira lies at the bottom of a valley, a huge peaceful beach reached along a dirt track, which attracts surfers throughout the year.

Beaches near Vila do Bispo North of Vila do Bispo, side roads lead off the N266 to the beaches around the little village of Carrapateira. Amado lures countless surfers, often taking part in competitions, while nearer the village, Bordeira is a wild, long, windswept beach, backed by dunes, with a little river, great for bathing at high tide. South lies Murração, beautiful, remote and unspoiled, with gentle green cliffs dropping to the sands. Nearer Bispo, there's a good tarmac road to Cordoama, a long, long beach at the foot of high cliffs. Nearby Castelejo is usually more crowded, but on this remote coast, remember all things are relative.

THE BASICS

⊞ B5
🍽 Summer restaurants and snack bars on some beaches; restaurants and bars in Vila do Bispo, Carapateira and Aljezur
♿ None
❓ The bathing is supervised on most of the west coast beaches between June and early September

More to See

ALJEZUR

On a site inhabited since prehistoric times, the little town of Aljezur was founded by the Moors, who built the castle here in the 10th century. It falls into three parts: the modern town on either side of the main coast road, the steep and narrow old town rising above, and the pleasant suburb of Igreja Nova across the river, named after its 'new' church, built after the 1755 earthquake. The ruins of the Moors' castle at the top of the old town can be reached by climbing up through the twisting cobbled streets. The views are superb in all directions. Downhill from the castle, Aljezur has a couple of low-key museums, the Casa José Cercas (Tue–Sat 10–1, 2–5.30), displaying works by a local artist, and the Museu Municipal (Tue–Sat 10–1, 2.30–5), devoted to archaeological finds from the area.

➕ C3 🍽 Restaurants, bars and cafés
🚌 Buses to Portimão and Lagos ♿ Few
ℹ Largo do Mercado, tel 282 998 229;
May–Sep Tue–Thu 9.30–7, Fri–Mon
9.30–1, 2–5.30; Oct–Apr Tue–Thu 9.30–5.30,
Fri–Mon 9.30–1, 2–5.30

BURGAU

Steep and narrow streets tumble down the hillside to the beach at Burgau, a laid-back and low-key resort-cum-fishing village west of Lagos. It has largely escaped excessive development, though new apartment blocks and villas are beginning to go up above the old town. Down by the beach where the fishing boats are drawn up, things remain unchanged, with a cluster of bars and restaurants overlooking the ideal family beach. It can get very crowded in high summer but outside these months Burgau is a reminder of how the Algarve used to be.

➕ C6 🍽 Restaurants and cafés 🚌 Buses
from Lagos ♿ Few

PRAIA DA LUZ

There's little sign of the original fishing village at Praia da Luz, beautifully set on shelving land west of Lagos. To the east of the sandy beach, cliffs rise up steeply, while westwards the sands merge into flat slabs of rock. A palm-lined promenade runs along the foreshore past the site of a Roman villa to the whitewashed 18th-century church and old fort, now a restaurant. Behind this modern Luz sprawls, an incohesive spread of low-rise apartment blocks, villas, shops, pools and tennis courts. It's a superb resort for families, best visited outside the high season when the beach is packed with day trippers from Lagos.

➕ D6 🍽 Restaurants and cafés 🚌 Buses
from Lagos ♿ Few

SALEMA

A winding road twists down a fertile and cultivated valley to Salema, an old fishing village that has mostly succeeded in holding back the tide of development that spreads west from Lagos. Boats are still hauled up on the beach and fishermen mend their nets on the town square behind, before climbing the steep cobbled streets to their traditional homes, many of them offering rooms to rent. Tourists here are mainly independent visitors, who come for the unspoiled atmosphere, the long stretch of clean sand, the great walking around the village and the good fish restaurants.

➕ C6 🍽 Restaurants and cafés 🚌 Buses
from Lagos ♿ Few

★

A Cliff Walk from Salema

This walk climbs up from Salema to head east over the cliffs to the isolated beach at Boca da Rio, at the foot of a gentle green valley.

DISTANCE: 3.5km (2 miles) **ALLOW:** Approximately 1 hour

START

SALEMA
✚ C6

END

BOCA DA RIO
✚ C6

❶ Start on the promenade at Salema, facing the sea. Turn left to head east along the promenade. Just past the bar Mira Mar, turn left uphill on the Travessa do Mar. At the top, turn right and climb up the cobbled street, lined with whitewashed houses, heading out of the village.

❻ Walk down to the beach; the buildings were associated with the tuna fishing industry and there are traces of a Roman villa; Boca da Rio was probably once a Roman fishing port.

❷ Continue until the end of the cobbled section and walk on until you're about 50m (55 yards) short of the road junction. Keep your eyes open for a sandy track on your right, heading steeply uphill towards the coast.

❺ After approximately 1km (0.6 miles) you'll see the beach at Boca da Rio below you and along the coast west as far as Sagres. Follow the cliff path down, joining the tarmac road to make your descent easier.

❹ Follow the line of the cliffs, with superb views along the coast opening up to the west and out to sea. Look out for birdlife and, in spring, the spreads of maritime flora. You should be able to spot wild thyme, cistus, pink convolvulus and the tiny, bright blue maritime pimpernel.

❸ Take this track and climb to the top of the cliff to join the stony path running parallel with the sea and head east (left).

A Drive up the West Coast

This circular drive travels up the west coast, exploring beaches and villages, before dropping south through fertile countryside.

DISTANCE: 103km (64 miles)   **ALLOW:** 2.5 hours or all day with stops

START → END

SAGRES
✚ A7

SAGRES

❶ From Sagres take the N268 north to Vila do Bispo. Continue all the way to Aljezur (36km/22.5 miles), perhaps stopping at some of the beaches (▷ 31) en route. The road runs north over windswept maquis and scrubland and past huge wind farms before giving way to rolling arable countryside, punctuated with stands of eucalyptus.

❼ Turn right at the traffic lights at Val de Boi and head west on the N125 to Vila do Bispo and back to Sagres.

❷ After visiting Aljezur (▷ 37), retrace your route south on the N268.

❻ Pass the Zoo entrance (4km/2.5 miles) and drive through the pretty village of São João, following the signs to Sagres and the *Mata Nacional*. The *Mata Nacional* (National Forest) is to your right; an area where the indigenous stone pines and other rare conifers are protected. After 6km (3.7 miles) the road runs through Barão São Miguel, then drops down through orchards of figs and almonds, particularly beautiful in spring, to the N125.

❸ After 9km (5.5 miles), bear right on to the N120 towards Bensafrim (signposted Faro and Lagos). The road runs over a ridge and down through cork oak woods on this lovely stretch of undulating country.

❹ At the roundabout, after 16km (10 miles), follow the signs to Bensafrim and drive through the village and over a bridge.

❺ Here, turn right to Barão de São João, go under the motorway and follow the signs to Zoo de Lagos.

Shopping

AMÓ

This huge store stocks an astonishing range of ceramics and pottery in all styles and at all prices. It's worth a long browse. They also sell souvenirs of every description.
✛ A7 ✉ Sitio do Tonel, Sagres ☎ 282 624 748

ANUSKA

This pretty store sells a wide range of bed linen and nightwear for women and children. There are lovely, delicate robes and wraps, flowered and striped sheets, bedcovers and cushions—all in finest Portuguese cotton.
✛ D6 ✉ Rua Garrett 8, Lagos ☎ 282 762 344

ARTESANATO MANFRED

An Aladdin's cave of a shop where jewellery and ornaments are made from polished stone and semi-precious jewels from all over the world. Earrings and necklaces are well-priced and the owner will make pieces for you on the spot.
✛ D6 ✉ Rua de São Gonçalo de Lagos 5, Lagos ☎ 969 228 991

CABO SÃO VICENTE

Just outside the lighthouse complex at Cape St. Vincent you'll find numerous stalls selling all manner of goods. This is the place to invest in a well-priced, hand-knitted sweater or wrap, gloves, scarves and hats,
local cured meat, honey and cheese and slippers.
✛ A7 ✉ Cabo de São Vicente

CASA DAS VERGAS

This lovely wood-lined shop sells artisan textiles made up into all manner of table linen, place mats and cloths, as well as thick woven Portuguese bath mats and a wide selection of attractive handmade basketry.
✛ D6 ✉ Rua 25 de Abril 77, Lagos ☎ 282 760028

COCO AND SHELLS

www.cocoshells.com
Pretty, feminine summertime jewellery is on offer here, with beads, shells, coconut shells, Amazon seeds and silver made up into affordable and individual necklaces, bracelets and earrings. Take your time browsing and if you can't find what you want, they will happily design and make something just for you. They also sell nice baskets and bags.
✛ D6 ✉ Largo da

SERVICE, PLEASE

It has to be said that service in Portuguese shops is not always good. Staff can be charming and helpful, but often are not, and you'll find a clear *'faz favor'* (please) may help you get some attention. The upside of this is that it's rare to be hassled so you can really take your time browsing.

Republica, Praia da Luz
☎ 933 440 033

GARDEUR DIRECT

www.gardeurdirect.com
A real find in the Algarve, this elegant shop specializes in women's wear, much of it by German designers. Beautiful and well-cut separates and knitwear are displayed, and they have a range of handmade jewellery and even stock genuine Panama hats.
✛ D6 ✉ Rua Direita, Praia da Luz ☎ 282 788 630

LAGOS SURF CENTER

www.lagossurfcenter.com
If you're heading west to surf, you can track down everything you need at this specialist store, which overhauls equipment and sells boards of all types by names such as Rip Curl, Reef, Billabong and Take Off, as well as surf fashion and wetsuits.
✛ D6 ✉ Rua Silva Lopes 31, Lagos ☎ 282 764 734

THOMAS GREEN

www.thomasgreen.pt
A friendly, English-run shop that specializes in imported British foods, ideal if you're self-catering. You'll find everything from Marmite through curry sauce and chocolate spread on the shelves and you can delve in the freezers for pies and ready-made meals.
✛ D6 ✉ Urbanzação Marina Sol, Lote 12, Loja A, Lagos ☎ 282 799 023

Entertainment and Activities

ALGARVE DOLPHINS
www.algarve-dolphins.com
High-speed RIBs take you out to sea on the trail of dolphins, with very high chances of spending time with a pod. There is a marine biologist to answer your questions and the guaranteed ticket option gives you a free follow-up trip if you don't find any dolphins.
➕ D6 ✉ Marina de Lagos 10, Lagos ☎ 282 764 144

BOM DIA
www.bomdia.info
This company runs fishing and sailing trips up and down the coast on its beautiful, three-sailed boats. You can take a coast trip to see the caves around Lagos or join one of the barbecue cruises, where there's a chance to swim, eat lunch and visit the caves.
➕ D6 ✉ Marina de Lagos 10, Lagos ☎ 282 087 587

CENTRO HIPICO QUINTA DO PARAÍSO ALTO
www.qpahorseriding.com
The instructors at this British-run riding outfit are all UK qualified, and organize many types of riding including 1-hour lessons, complete courses, moonlight rides and trips to restaurants on horseback. They have horses to suit every level of expertise.
➕ D6 ✉ Fronteira, Bensafrim, Lagos ☎ 282 687 596/282 789 801

GRAND CAFÉ
This wonderful, high-ceilinged building is considered by locals to be the coolest night spot in Lagos. Opening at 7 or 8 every evening, things get going around midnight and continue until 4am. There are guest DJs at weekends.
➕ D6 ✉ Rua Senhora da Graça 7, Lagos

MARILIMITADO
www.marilimitado.com
An experienced group of marine biologists run trips from Sagres up the west coast to see whales, dolphins, seabirds and turtles. They use RIBs, speak excellent English, and can take you to swim with wild dolphins.
➕ A7 ✉ Porto da Baleeira, Sagres ☎ 916 832 625

PARQUE DA FLORESTA
www.parquedafloresta.com
The most westerly golf course in the Algarve is part of the sports complex attached to a

---

THE BIG OUTDOORS

If you enjoy the wilder side of the great outdoors the western Algarve is the best destination; there's a plethora of activities on offer. The whole of the west coast is a designated natural park, ensuring that flora, fauna and marine life are heavily protected and that the entire area will remain undeveloped.

---

tourist development, so there's also a spa, tennis and bowls on offer. The 18-hole course is hilly and challenging, with views towards the coast.
➕ C6 ✉ Vale de Poço, Budens ☎ 282 690 054

SAGRES NATURA
www.sagresnatura.com
A multilingual, young team run this friendly company that offers a great range of sporting excursions—choose from exploring the sea caves by canoe, surfing and body-boarding or mountain-biking.
➕ A7 ✉ Rua Mestre Antonio Galhardo, Sagres ☎ 282 624 072

STEVIE RAY'S
www.stevie-rays.com
Lagos' most popular live music bar is open every night, but the music and atmosphere are best at weekends, when there are blues and jazz bands.
➕ D6 ✉ Rua Senhora da Graça 9, Lagos ☎ 914 923 883/914 923 885

ZOO DE LAGOS
www.zoolagos.com
This environmentally conscious zoo has enough to keep the kids happy for an hour or so. It's attractively laid out to allow a good chance of getting up close to the animals. There's a restaurant, shop and children's playground.
➕ C5 ✉ Sítio do Medronhal, Barão de S João, Lagos ☎ 282 680 100

Restaurants

A TASCA (€)

The best fish restaurant in Sagres overlooks the harbour, where the fish on your plate is landed daily. Sit outside on the terrace or in the cosy interior. The seafood and fish couldn't be fresher, plus you'll also find a few meat dishes and a good wine list featuring wines from the Alentejo.

🔢 A7 ✉ Porto da Baleeira, Sagres ☎ 282 624 177 🕙 Thu–Tue lunch and dinner

A VACA (€€)

This intimate restaurant serves a taste of Switzerland in the shape of fondue, *raclette* (melted cheese with potatoes and cured ham), creamy potato and cheese gratin and some plainly grilled steak. Swiss and German beers are on offer as well as a full wine list.

🔢 D6 ✉ Rua Silva Lopes, Lagos ☎ 282 761 022 🕙 Daily lunch and dinner, closed Sun

ADEGA DO PAPAGAIO (€€)

It's worth the drive out from Lagos for the evening to this lively restaurant, where the set menu includes as much as you can eat of seven varieties of meat, cooked on a stone grill—and it's you that does the cooking, adding to the fun. There's usually live music, which occasionally features *fado*, Portugal's soul music.

🔢 D6 ✉ Espiche (5 km/ 3 miles west of Lagos) ☎ 282 789 423 🕙 Daily lunch and dinner

BEACH BAR (€€)

On the beach at Burgau, this friendly fish restaurant doubles as a popular bar, where you can sit on the terrace to either eat or drink. The menu is Portuguese, with fresh fish and grills, all served with plenty of accompaniments. Booking is advised for dinner.

🔢 C6 ✉ Praia de Burgau ☎ 282 697 553 🕙 Tue–Sun lunch and dinner

BOIA BAR (€€)

www.boiabar.com

This airy, spacious bar-restaurant has its feet on the sand on Salema beach and is open for everything from breakfast to late-night supper. All fish is sourced from Sagres along the coast, and the chef will happily prepare it 'English-style'—without the head and tail. The menu also includes snacks, pasta dishes and a mean chicken piri-piri.

🔢 C6 ✉ Rua dos Pescadores 101, Salema ☎ 282 695 382 🕙 Apr–Sep daily 10–midnight; Oct–Mar Thu–Tue 10–midnight

ESTRELA DO MAR (€€€)

Climb up above Lagos' main market building to this excellent fish restaurant, where you can take in the same sweeping views. The food has a decidedly Mediterranean twist, using plenty of herbs and fresh vegetables in its imaginatively cooked fish dishes. For something truly Portuguese, the *cataplana* is recommended.

🔢 D6 ✉ Mercado Municipal, Lagos ☎ 282 769 250 🕙 Lunch Tue–Sat, dinner Mon–Sat

FORTALEZA DA LUZ (€€–€€€)

www.fortalezadaluz.com

Luz's most up-market restaurant is housed in the town's atmospheric 16th-century fortress,

beautifully set in gardens overlooking the sea. There's a marked contrast between the lunch and dinner menus, but you'll find international as well as Portuguese specialties, though don't expect anything cutting-edge. The menu specializes in fish, but there are also meat, pasta and vegetarian dishes. At Sunday lunch there is a barbecue and live jazz.

➕ D6 ✉ Rua da Igreja 3, Praia da Luz ☎ 282 789 926/282 788 993 🕐 Daily lunch and dinner; closed mid-Nov to mid-Dec

MAR Á VISTA (€€)

Set above one of Sagres' beaches, the Mar á Vista has a lovely terrace overlooking the sea and a cosy interior. You can choose from a long menu of good-value fish and chicken, all served in enormous quantities, or opt for a simple omelette or salad.

➕ A7 ✉ Sítio da Mareta, Sagres ☎ 282 624 247 🕐 Thu–Tue lunch and dinner

MEMMO BALEEIRA SAGRES (€€€)

A modern, stylish restaurant in an equally stylish hotel that offers great views across the harbour at Sagres. Chef Miguel Raimundo sources as much as possible locally, then combines his ingredients in a Portuguese-Mediterranean fusion menu, with the accent on

clean, clear flavours, with a plentiful use of herbs. There is an excellent wine list and highly attentive service—a real treat for a big night out.

➕ A7 ✉ Memmo Baleeira Hotel, Sagres ☎ 282 624 212 🕐 Daily dinner

MIRA MAR (€–€€)

This simple bar-cum-restaurant is perched right beside Salema's beachside promenade and offers well-priced, simply grilled fish washed down with some excellent house *sangria*.

➕ C6 ✉ Travessa do Mar 6, Salema ☎ 919 560 339 🕐 Daily lunch and dinner

NORTADA (€–€€)

Named after a local trade wind that draws windsurfers from all over Europe, this restaurant has a wonderful beachfront location.

INTERNATIONAL EATING

There's a wealth of international restaurants in the Algarve, often run by natives of the countries whose food features. Albufeira in particular has many British eating places, so if you're pining for a Sunday roast, here's your chance. Most resorts, no matter how small, will have a Chinese or Indian restaurant, and you can also find food from all over the Mediterranean, Germany and even Switzerland.

There's plenty of super-fresh fish on the menu of Portuguese specialities, which include an excellent *cataplana*, oysters, and even barnacles for the adventurous diner. Or you could have a pizza.

➕ A7 ✉ Praia do Martinhal, Sagres ☎ 918 613 410 🕐 Jul–Oct daily lunch and dinner, Nov–Jun daily lunch

O ARTISTA (€–€€)

You can come here from morning till after midnight for a drink, a snack or a full meal. The menu features all the usual Portuguese dishes, with some international ones as well, but the chief draw for most diners is the nightly entertainment, which ranges from a quiz night (in English) on Tuesday, through to 60s music and karaoke.

➕ D6 ✉ Rua António Crisóquno dos Santos, Lagos ☎ 282 769 147 🕐 Daily 10.30–2am

VILA VELHA (€€€)

This traditional, white-washed house, set in a pretty garden, is home to one of Sagres' best restaurants, where traditional Portuguese dishes are given a modern twist. There's usually a couple of vegetarian options, a children's menu and some delicious puddings. Booking is advised.

➕ A7 ✉ Rua Patrão Faustino, Sagres ☎ 282 624 788 🕐 Feb–Nov Tue–Sun dinner

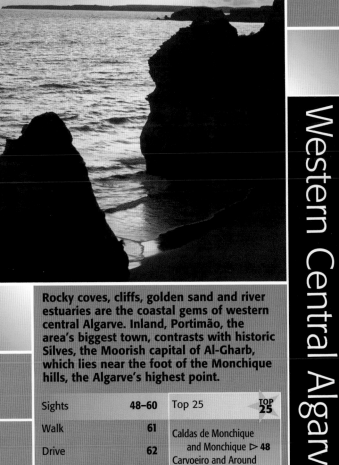

Rocky coves, cliffs, golden sand and river estuaries are the coastal gems of western central Algarve. Inland, Portimão, the area's biggest town, contrasts with historic Silves, the Moorish capital of Al-Gharb, which lies near the foot of the Monchique hills, the Algarve's highest point.

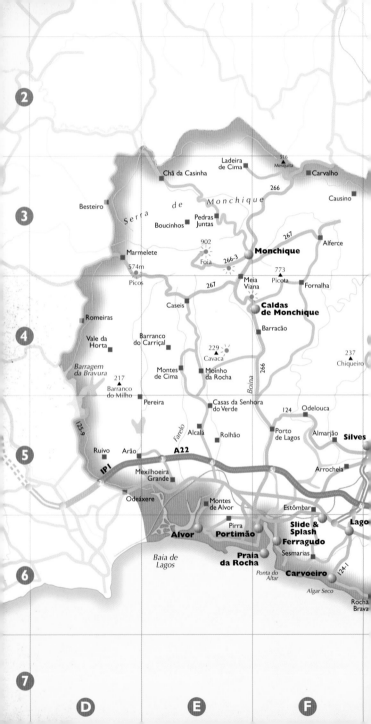

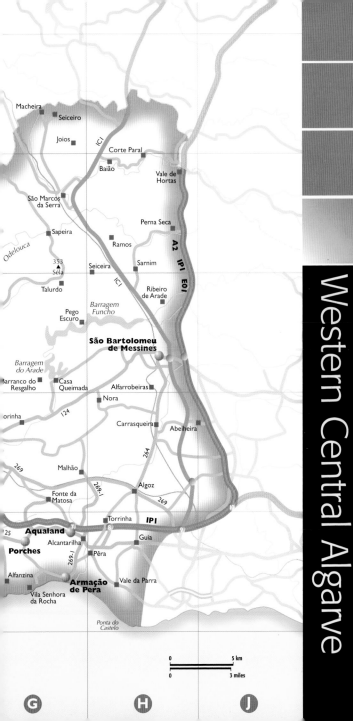

Macheira

Seiceiro

Joios

ICI

Corte Paral

Baião

Vale de
Hortas

São Marcos
da Serra

Perna Seca

Sapeira

A2

Ramos

Odelouca

Seiceira

Sarnim

IP1

EO1

353
Séla

ICI

Talurdo

Ribeiro
de Arade

Pego
Escuro

Barragem
Funcho

São Bartolomeu
de Messines

Barragem
do Arade

Barranco do
Resgalho

Casa
Queimada

Alfarrobeiras

Nora

orinha

124

Carrasqueira

Abelheira

264

269

Malhão

269-1

Algoz

Fonte da
Matosa

269

Torrinha

IP1

10

25

Aqualand

8

9

Porches

Alcantarilha

269-1

Guia

Pêra

Alfanzina

Vale da Parra

**Armação
de Pera**

Vila Senhora
da Rocha

Ponta do
Castelo

0   5 km
0   3 miles

G   H   J

Caldas de Monchique and Monchique

HIGHLIGHTS

- The central square at Caldas de Monchique
- The Moorish-inspired casino
- The 19th-century buildings
- The gardens and wooded walks

TIPS

- You can use the spa even if you aren't staying.
- Visit Monchique town on a Sunday morning when local farmers set up a market selling fresh produce.

The Algarve's best-known spa, the Caldas de Monchique, is a cluster of charming Edwardian buildings set in a high wooded valley. From here, the road ascends to the little agricultural town of Monchique, a world away from the seaside resorts.

Caldas de Monchique Twenty million litres of water, at a temperature of 32°C (90°F), gush out annually from the springs at Monchique, supplying both a bottling plant, and a spa, where visitors come for thermal treatments for rheumatism and respiratory ailments. The Romans came here first and called the site Mons Cicus, but the Caldas owe their present appearance to the 19th-century enthusiasm for 'taking the waters', when the rich bourgeoisie flocked here to lodge in the purpose-built spa buildings. Today, it's had

Clockwise from left: Handicrafts in Monchique; orange groves in the Serra de Monchique; small church at Caldas de Monchique; view of the spa village of Caldas de Monchique; traditional pottery for sale; the fountain in the middle of Monchique

a recent makeover, and the old casino, inn and bars make a pleasant spot to relax before strolling through the lovely woods that surround the Caldas. You can taste the distinctly sulphurous waters at the treatment complex, also the place to book a session at the baths (tel 282 910 910).

Monchique Further up the hill, Monchique town, situated at an altitude of 458m (1,502ft), is a no-nonsense hill settlement, with a pretty square, complete with a fountain inspired by a traditional *nora* (Algarve well), and the lovely 16th-century Igreja Matriz. You can buy delicious local pork products in its shops, and its craftsmen still turn out unique folding wooden chairs, whose design is said to have been invented by the Romans. From here, the road leads up through woods to Foia (902m/2,958ft), the highest point in the Algarve.

THE BASICS

www.monchiquetermas. com
www.monchiqueportugal. com
✚ F4 (Caldas de Monchique);
E3 (Monchique)
🍴 Restaurants, bars and cafés in Monchique and Caldas de Monchique
🚌 Buses from Portimão
♿ Few, though good in spa
ℹ Largo São Sebastão, tel 282 911 189; daily 9.30–1, 2–5.30

Carvoeiro and Around

White houses cluster round a sheltered cove at Carvoeiro, 30 years ago an un-spoiled fishing village east of Portimão. Today, its chief catch is tourists, who flock here for the idyllic beaches, steep cliffs and plethora of accommodation.

Carvoeiro Village Turn off the N125, follow the valley towards the sea, and you'll find the road ends in the heart of the village: a little square beside the beach, where there are still a few fishing boats pulled up on the sand. Dazzlingly white houses tumble down towards the sea on either side, many of them now housing bars, shops and restaurants, while away from the old village, low-rise development stretches in either direction along the coast and back inland. This is a good place to catch a boat to the beaches east of here,

Clockwise from top left: The lovely cove at Carvoeiro; fishing boats pulled up on to the beach; a view of the dramatic coastline; pretty white houses in Carvoeiro; a rock formation in the sea just off shore; a fishing boat with a painted-eye design

take a trip to view the rock formations in the cliffs, or simply relax on the beach or browse in the dozens of holiday shops.

The Beaches A string of beaches stretches east of Carvoeiro, all offering the essentials of high sheltering cliffs and golden sands. Algar Seco, with its weird rock formations and crystalline waters, draws the crowds, or head further to Centianes, a beautiful cove reached by steps down the high cliffs. There's a tourist train from Carvoeiro to Algar Seco and Centianes from May to September. Further east still is Praia do Carvalho, reached by a tunnel entrance and known as the Smuggler's Beach, while east again you reach Praia da Marinha, perhaps the best of the lot, with arches, caves and rock formations that are home to varied marine life and a big attraction for snorkellers.

THE BASICS

➕ F6

🍴 Restaurants, bars and cafés

🚌 Buses from Portimão

♿ Few

❓ Nearby: Ferraguda, Lagoa, Porches and Armação de Pera

ℹ️ Praia do Carvoeiro, tel 282 357 728; May–Sep Tue–Thu 9.30–7, Fri–Mon 9.30–1, 2–5.30; Oct–Apr daily 9.30–5.30

Portimão

TIPS

● Parking is difficult; the best places are on Rua Serpa Pinto near the river, or out near the football stadium on the Praia da Rocha road.
● Portimão shops have a fair selection, but you'll find better shopping at the Algarve's malls (▷ 12).
● There's a daily market on Avenida São João de Deus.
● The gypsy market takes place on the 1st and 3rd Mondays of the month, and the flea market takes place on the 1st and 3rd Sundays.

Big and bustling, Portimão is the Algarve's most functional town, busy with its own, quite separate, life, well away from the tourists. Come here to taste this side of the Algarve, and enjoy the buzz of a thriving community.

The Town The Romans called the town Portus Magnus, and history's spotlight touched it in 1487, when Bartolomeu Dias set off from here to become the first European to round the Cape of Good Hope. It was a thriving port town, whose prosperity was severely checked by the 1755 earthquake. This destroyed much of Portimão, explaining the dearth of old buildings in the town today. One of the oldest is the lovely church of Nossa Senhora da Conceição, rebuilt after the earthquake, but retaining its Manueline doorway

Clockwise from left: Suspension bridge over the River Arade; detail of the decoration on the prow of a boat; view of a fort from across the river in Portimão; various boat trips set sail from Portimão; azulejos decorate a bench in Largo 1 de Dezembro

and covered inside with 17th-century *azulejos*. You'll find more of these lovely tiles, depicting Portuguese historical scenes, inlaid on benches in the Largo 1 de Dezembro, a pretty square just off the pedestrian-only shopping streets of Rua Diogo Tomé and Rua da Portades de São José.

The Riverfront From the Largo 1 de Dezembro it's a few steps to the riverfront, the most attractive area of the town, laid out in a series of garden squares, with cafés beneath the trees. The marina is sited here, and it's also the departure point for the boat trips that run up the River Arade to Carvoeiro, Lagos and upriver to Silves. Further upstream, the mouth-watering aroma of freshly grilled sardines permeates the air from the open-air restaurants, near the old fishing quarter, that cluster round the hidden square of Largo da Barca.

THE BASICS

➕ F6

🍴 Restaurants, bars and cafés

🚌 Buses from Lagos, Lagoa, Praia da Rocha, Carvoeiro

🚏 Largo Ferra Prado

ℹ️ Avenida Zeca Afonso, tel 282 470 717; daily 9.30–5.30. Closed public holidays

Praia da Rocha

HIGHLIGHTS

● Rock formations–the
Three Bears, the Lion Rock
and the Two Brothers
● View of the river from
the *fortaleza*

TIPS

● To escape the worst development and commercialism,
stick to the east end of both
the town and beach.
● You can walk along the
beach on a boardwalk–ideal
in summer when the sand's
too hot for bare feet.

**The Algarve's oldest resort, Praia da
Rocha pulls in the crowds who come to
idle away the days on its superb south-
facing, cliff-backed beach and enjoy the
impressive tourist infrastructure of hotels,
apartments, restaurants and nightlife.**

Origins Holidaymakers discovered Praia da
Rocha over a century ago, when foreign intellectu-
als wintered here and spread the word of its beautiful beach and mild climate. By the 1950s and
'60s it was booming, quickly earning the name
'Queen of the Algarve', its main street lined with
elegant villas and sophisticated hotels. Those days
are long gone, and this famous holiday resort is
now largely given over to high-rise hotels, faceless
apartment blocks, home-from-home bars and
eating houses, and discos.

Clockwise from left: The cliff-backed beach at Praia da Rocha features striking rock formations; a row of hotels behind the sandy beach; striking white and blue buildings; a view of the marina from the Fortaleza de Santa Catarina

The Resort Today Nothing though, can detract from the dramatic rock formations and the glorious beach, the widest cliff-backed stretch in Europe. It was created in 1969 when just under one million metric tonnes of sand were moved here, pushing the sea back some 150m (164 yards) and leaving the rock stacks, formerly lapped by water, high and dry. Access to this wonder is down steep steps from various points along the Avenida Tomás Cabreira. This road runs along the cliff top from the Fortaleza de Santa Catarina, built in 1691 to protect the river mouth—it's a great place to watch the fishing boats come in or take in the sunset. You can walk down the Avenida to admire the few remaining turn-of-the-century villas, relics of the days when Praia da Rocha was a hot-bed of international intrigue and fast living. Here too you'll find countless bars, shops and restaurants.

THE BASICS

+ F6
* Restaurants, bars and cafés
* Buses from Portimão
* Stones can fall from the cliffs so take care when walking beneath them. Do not venture too close to the edge of the cliff top. Portimão, Alvor are nearby
* Avenida Tomás Cabreira, tel 282 419 132; May–Sep daily 9.30–7; Oct–Apr daily 9.30–5.30

Silves

HIGHLIGHTS

● Praça do Municípo
● Sé
● Castelo
● Igreja da Misericórdia
● Museu Arqueológico
● Roman bridge
● Fabrica Inglês
● Caminho do Garb (Islamic Heritage Centre)

Steeped in history, the inland town of Silves, dominated by its castle and set on the banks of the River Arade, combines a tranquil setting, homogenous architecture and plenty of sightseeing with a very special and relaxed atmosphere.

A Bit of History Silves, Moorish Xelb, was the Islamic capital of Al-Gharb, a major fortress, river port and commercial hub, whose wealth and influence was renowned all over Europe. After the 13th-century expulsion of the Moors, the town declined, the river silted up and by the 16th century Silves was a forgotten backwater, its population, once over 30,000, shrunk to 150 inhabitants. Cork processing revived it in the 19th century and today Silves thrives on tourism, citrus-growing and farming.

Clockwise from left: The interior of the Gothic Sé; a statue of a knight in the grounds of the castle; a view of the red-tiled roofs of Silves beneath the castle; the town's pretty main square; a 12th-century Moorish well in the Museu Arqueológico; the castle walls

Exploring Silves Inland, head for the Largo dos Municipios and the Caminho do Garb (Islamic Heritage Centre; Mon–Fri 9–5; free), which traces Silves' Moorish history. From here, cobbled streets head steeply uphill to the Castle (daily 9–6.30; inexpensive). Climb the walls for magnificent views before exploring the Arab cistern, baths and restored interior gardens. Just outside is the Sé (Mon–Fri 3–5; inexpensive), a twin-towered Gothic church, built on the site of the Mosque and the Algarve's main cathedral until 1577. Downhill is the Museu Arqueológico (Mon–Sat 9–6; inexpensive), tracing local history through Phoenician, Roman and Moorish times. The Fabrica Inglês (daily 9–midnight; free), the town's old cork factory now revamped as a cultural-cum-leisure complex, lies near the river, where there's a lively morning market.

THE BASICS

🚹 G5
🍴 Restaurants, bars and cafés
🚌 Buses from Portimão and Lagoa
🚉 2km (1.2 miles) south of Silves and connected by bus
♿ Few
ℹ En 124, Parque das Merendas, tel 282 442 511; May–Sep Mon–Fri 9.30–7; Oct–Apr Mon–Fri 9.30–1, 2–5

Water Parks

TOP 25

There's plenty of fun to be had at the Algarve's water parks

THE BASICS

Aqualand
www.aqualand.pt
🔲 G6
✉ Sítio das Areiras, Alcantarilha
☎ 282 320 230
🕐 Jun–second week Sep daily 10–6
🍴 Restaurant, café and self-service cafeteria (€–€€)
🚌 Bus shuttle service from most of the main resorts
♿ None
💷 Expensive

Slide & Splash
www.slidesplash.com
🔲 F6
✉ Estrada Nacional 125, Vale de Deus, Estombar
☎ 282 340 800
🕐 6 Apr–May, 19 Sep–30 Oct daily 10–5, Jun, 1–18 Sep daily 10–5.30, Jul–Aug daily 10–6
🍴 Restaurants and fast-food kiosks (€–€€)
🚌 Bus shuttle service from most of the main resorts
♿ None
💷 Expensive

TIP

● Bus companies in main tourist centres may offer money-saving bus plus admission packages.

Long hot summer days are the ideal time to head for one of the Algarve's water parks, where the whole family can keep cool, let off steam, and try out some of Europe's longest and scariest flumes and water rides.

Aqualand Once aptly named The Big One, Aqualand, with some of the scariest slides around, is a good bet for older kids. The big attractions are the Banzai Boggan, where you drop 23m (75ft) on a surfboard, and the Kamikaze, where you'll soar 36m (118ft) above ground before descending with stomach churning speed in four seconds flat. This is possibly outclassed by the Anaconda, a collection of snaking tubes dropping at vertiginous angles into a pool. Add on some slide lanes, a turbulent ride known as the Rapids, a shallow, safe play area for small children, and a huge pool and you've got all the ingredients for what many kids see as the highlight of their holiday.

Slide & Splash Advertising itself as 'the best waterpark in Europe', Slide & Splash, has been pulling in the crowds since 1986, and every year sees the introduction of new rides and the over-hauling of others. Dotted about a huge grassy area are slides for all ages, ranging from the precipitous drop of the Kamikaze and the adrenalin surge of the Black Hole—where you zoom down in total darkness—to the less daunting plunge pools and wide slide lanes. Small children are well provided for with a water play area where they can try the elephant slides, tunnels and water spitting dragon.

More to See

ALVOR

One of the Algarve's few undiscovered gems, Alvor is a picturesque and traditional town, with a lovely position on a river estuary, fabulous beaches nearby and some of the best fish restaurants for miles around. These are clustered round the harbour itself, and the scent of grilled sardines mingles with that of the sea. From here, a tangle of cobbled streets leads uphill to the fine 16th-century Igreja Matriz and the castle ruins. From the harbour you can walk upriver or head left for ten minutes to reach the sweeping, safe, sandy beach.

➕ E6 🍴 Restaurants, bars and cafés 🚌 Buses from Portimão ♿ Beach classified as suitable for disabled access ❱ Rua Dr Afonso Costa 51, tel 282 457 540; Mon–Fri 9.30–1, 2–5.30 (times may vary)

ARMAÇÃO DE PERA

Firmly Portuguese, the resort of Armação has one of the longest and best beaches in the Algarve, where the fishermen from inland Pera set their nets and launched their boats. There are still a few left, and the old nucleus of the modern town, all whitewashed houses and cobbled streets, still huddles round the Praia dos Pescadores, the Fishermen's Beach. Modern Armação is a resort town, with high-rise apartments and economical hotels; its main attraction is its Portuguese atmosphere. There are boat trips from the town along the west coast to see rocks and caves.

➕ G6 🍴 Restaurants, bars and cafés 🚌 Buses to Albufeira, Portimão and Silves ❱ Avenida Marginal, tel 282 312 145; May–Sep Fri–Mon 9.30–1, 2–5.30, Tue–Thu 9.30–7; Oct–Apr Fri–Mon 9.30–1, 2–5.30, Tue–Thu 9.30–5.30

FERRAGUDO

Set on a little river running into the estuary of the River Arade, Ferragudo curves around a strip of gardens, its focus the cobbled square of Praça Rainha Dona Leonor. It's a beguiling place, one of the Algarve's least spoiled former fishing villages, all whitewashed houses, many of which

A detail from inside the 16th-century church in the traditional town of Alvor

The sandy beach at Armação de Pera is one of the Algarve's best beaches

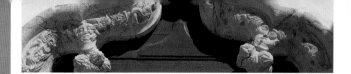

are owned as holiday homes by wealthy Lisboans. Their presence has preserved the traditional character of Ferragudo, seen at its best in the flower-hung streets running uphill to the church—there's a great view across to Portimão from its terrace. The town beach is overlooked by a castle, half of the pair built to defend the River Arade—the other is in Praia da Rocha (▷ 54).

➕ F6 🍴 Restaurants, bars and cafés
🚌 Buses from Portimão

LAGOA

Just off the N125, Lagoa is a down-to-earth town, largely untouched by the tourism at nearby Carvoeiro (▷ 50). It's noted for its wine—you'll see vineyards in the surrounding countryside—which is produced at a large co-operative on the main road; there are tastings at the factory shop. The heart of the old town is an attractive mix of narrow streets, white houses and cobbled squares.

➕ F6 🍴 Restaurants, bars and cafés
🚌 Buses from Portimão

PORCHES

The name Porches is synonymous with pottery, for it was here that Patrick Swift, an Irish potter, and Lima de Freitas, a Portuguese artist, settled in the early 1960s intent on reviving the dying local pottery tradition. They founded the Olaria de Porches, still going strong, and its presence drew other potters to the area and helped preserve interest in traditional pottery throughout the Algarve. Porches today has several outlets in the village and beside the N125.

➕ G6 🍴 Cafés and restaurants 🚌 Buses from Portimão

SÃO BARTOLOMEU DE MESSINES

If you're driving from Silves (▷ 56) to Alte (▷ 72), it's worth making a stop in São Bartolomeu, a large village set in agricultural countryside. The church here is a beautiful 16th-century building with rope-twisted Manueline columns and glowing 17th-century glazed *azulejos* inside.

➕ H4 🍴 Cafés 🚌 Buses from Albufeira, Portimão and Silves

The restored baroque façade of the Igreja Matriz in Lagoa

Pottery urns for sale outside a shop in Porches

A Walk around Historic Silves

Wend your way up and downhill, to find the historic heart of Silves before wandering through the lower town to the riverside.

DISTANCE: 1.3km (0.8 miles) **ALLOW:** 45 minutes; 1–2 hours with visits and stops

START

PRAÇA DO MUNICÍPIO
🞦 G5

1 In Praça do Município, with your back to the road, turn right under the arch and bear left to head up Rua da Sé. The street widens at the top into the Largo Jerónimo Osório and ahead of you on the left is the ex-church of the Misericórdia, now a space for changing art exhibitions.

2 Climb further to the Sé, on your right, which backs on to the approach to the Castelo.

3 Leave the Castelo and bear right uphill past the bar and craft shop. At the top, there are views over the valley towards the river. Walk straight on and down the Rua Porta da Azóia, ignoring the left hand turn until you come to the top of the cobbled Rua Afonso III.

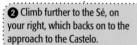

END

PONTE ROMANA
🞦 G5

7 Exit at the bottom gate and cross the road to the riverside, walking past the gardens and cafés until you reach the Roman bridge on your left.

6 Take the fifth turning right and you'll see the Fabrica Inglês on your left.

5 Turn right and continue downhill to emerge on the terrace overlooking the Praça do Município. Turn left from the *praça* into Rua Dr Francisco Vieira and walk along to its continuation, Rua Candido dos Reis.

4 Branch left here into Rua da Mascarenhas, which drops downhill, passing a section of the Moorish walls and a watch tower on your right. At the bottom turn left with a view to the Sé ahead; below you you'll see the back of the imposing 18th-century Camâra Municipal.

A Drive through the Hills

This drive into the hills from Portimão includes lovely woods, a spa village and sweeping views over the whole of the western Algarve.

DISTANCE: 62km (38.5 miles)   **ALLOW:** 1.5 hours driving; 3.5 hours with stops

❶ On the N125, cross the River Arade by road bridge—look out for the storks' nests on top—and, after 1.5km (0.9 miles), follow the blue signs to Monchique and the A22 motorway. At the roundabout giving access to the motorway come off the N125 and join the N124, passing underneath the motorway and following the signs to Monchique.

❷ Continue on this road, running up the valley of the River Boina, for 5km (3 miles) to Porto de Lagos.

❸ Bear left here onto the N266 signed Monchique. This road gradually climbs into the Monchique hills, the fertile fields giving way to mixed woodland, and views opening up. After 11km (7 miles) turn left on to the narrow side road signposted Caldas de Monchique; drive down to park in the town while you explore.

❼ Turn left here back on the N124 and continue on this road, rich in orange groves, for 11km (7 miles) to reach Silves.

❻ Retrace your route through Monchique and back to the junction with the N124 at Porto de Lagos.

❺ Leaving town, follow the main road from the main square to take the uphill right hand turn onto the Foia road. Follow this beautiful road through the woods and up to the summit, with ever-widening views to the coast opening up as you climb.

❹ Leaving Caldas de Monchique, return to the N266 further downhill from the entrance. Turn left and continue upwards to Monchique.

Shopping

CASA DOS ARCOS
Monchique is the place to buy the wooden folding chairs you see all round Portugal. The X-shaped design was brought to Portugal by the Romans and these alder-wood chairs have been made in Monchique for nearly 2,000 years. Tables and stools are also on offer at the 'Chairman of Monchique'.
➕ E3 ✉ Estrada Velha, Monchique ☎ 282 911 071

CASA J A MAIO
Opposite the 'Chairman' in Monchique you'll find this huge store, which, as well as local chairs and baskets, stocks artisan handworks from all over Portugal—check out the ceramics and slippers from the Alentejo.
➕ E3 ✉ Estrada Velha, Monchique ☎ 282 912 452

GUIA ALGARVE SHOPPING MALL
www.algarveshopping.pt
A huge mall with excellent children's facilities, which include free pushchairs and pedal cars as well as a crèche. Shops include Zara, Massimo Dutti and Pepe Jeans; there's a cinema, food court and covered parking.
➕ H6 ✉ On N125 outside Albufeira ☎ 282 105 500
🕐 Daily 10am–11pm

LOJO DE PORCO PRETO
In Portugal, ham and other pork products

traditionally come from the hills, and this high-quality shop is an outlet for the local producers of Monchique. You can buy fresh pork, but the main draw are the delicious *presuntos* (cured mountain ham) and the range of sausages and blood puddings.
➕ E3 ✉ Rua Serpa Pinto 18, Monchique ☎ 282 913 461

MERCADO VELHA
Carvoeiro's old food market is now the venue for a range of outlets selling handicrafts and decorative Portuguese pottery and ceramics. You can browse for jewellery and beachwear, or choose a take-home souvenir from the wide selection of knick-knacks, plates, bowls and table accessories.
➕ F6 ✉ Rua dos Pescadores, Carvoeiro

POTTERY
The Moors brought the art of pottery-making to the Algarve and the tradition continues. You'll find road-side pottery outlets everywhere, selling hand-painted jugs, plates and bowls, pots for the garden and the beautiful panels of *azulejos* (tiles). Prices vary considerably, but bear in mind you're paying for a genuine, hand-made object. The more up-market outlets will arrange shipping if you're buying in bulk.

OLARIA DE PORCHES
www.porchespottery.com
The Porches pottery (on the south side of the N125, ▷ 60) specializes in hand-thrown, hand-decorated ceramics, as well as beautiful *azulejos*. You can watch the pottery being decorated, before browsing the showrooms, where there's everything from egg-cups to bowls.
➕ G6 ✉ Estrada Nacional 125 Alqueves, Porches ☎ 282 352 858 🍴 On-site café

OLARIA PEQUENA
www.olariapequena.com
Glowing hues and bold, traditionally inspired modern designs are the hallmarks of the beautiful pieces sold at the Olaria Pequena (on the north side of the N125). The potters are Ian Fitzpatrick and Marco Correia, who specialize in one-off commissions, particularly panels of *azulejos*.
➕ G6 ✉ Estrada Nacional 125, Porches ☎ 282 381 213

QUINTA DO MIRADOURO
www.winesvidanova.com
Fans of Sir Cliff Richard come to the singer's wine estate, part of the Miradouro co-operative, which produces increasingly respected wines. You can take a vineyard tour and enjoy a tasting, but the main draw is the Cellar Door shop.
➕ H6 ✉ Quinta do Miradouro, Guia (off N125 to south) ☎ 968 776 971

Entertainment and Activities

ALTO GOLF

www.altoclub.com

In rolling countryside with views to the sea and Portimão, this Henry Cotton-designed 18-hole course is testing, featuring Europe's longest par 5. With chipping and putting greens, you can hire buggies. A handicap certificate is required.

🚩 E6 ✉ Quinta do Alto do Paço, Alvor ☎ 282 460 870

ARADE MAR

Cruise up the River Arade from Portimão to Silves in a gaily painted, traditionally designed river boat. The return cruise also allows an hour for exploring Silves.

🚩 F6 ✉ Rua Serpa Pinto 19, Portimão ☎ 282 419 998

CARVOEIRO CLUBE DE TÉNIS

www.tenniscarvoeiro.com

There are 12 courts, floodlit after dark, in this welcoming club, which runs tennis camps and tournaments throughout the year. The complex has a good-sized gym, with expert advice on hand and there are aerobics, exercise and dance classes, a swimming pool and snack bar and café.

🚩 F6 ✉ Mato Serrão, Carvoeiro ☎ 282 357 847

CRUZEIROS SANTA BERNARDA

www.santa-bernarda.com

This *caravela*, a replica of the 15th-century boats designed in Portugal for exploration, runs coastal cruises from Portimão. Dropping anchor at some of the most dramatic of the coastal caves and rock formations, you have a chance to explore them from the water. There are also full-day excursions, with barbecue included, which tour the coast and offer time for sunbathing and a swim.

🚩 F6 ✉ Rua Júdice Fialho, 4, Portimão ☎ 282 422 791 (and fax); Mobile: +351 967 023 840

DIVERS COVE

www.diverscove.de

This registered PADI dive outfit offers accompanied dives up and down the coast. Beginners and experts are equally welcome, and you can explore the sea caves, examine marine life and dive by day and night from their well-equipped dive boats.

🚩 F6 ✉ Quinta do Paraiso, Carvoeiro ☎ 282 356 594

DOLPHIN SEAFARIS

www.dolphinseafaris.com

Rigid inflatables with powerful onboard motors are used by this friendly company operating out of both Portimão and Lagos. The trips, lasting about an hour and a half, run up and down the coast in search of dolphins, whales and sharks.

🚩 F6 ✉ Marina de Portimão ☎ 282 799 209; Mobile: +351 918 704 267

HOTEL ALGARVE CASINO

www.solverde.pt

Portugal's original casino is housed in Praia da Rocha's grandest hotel, overlooking the beach. Blackjack and roulette are the main table games; there's also a huge room with 336 state-of-the-art slot machines. There are floorshows and live music.

🚩 F6 ✉ Avenida Tomá Cabreira, Praia da Rocha ☎ 282 402 000 🕐 4pm–4am (some days 3pm–3am). Table games 8.30pm–3/4am

JAILHOUSE

Established in the 1960s, the Jailhouse hosted big names of pop, rock and jazz. The clientele span all ages and in between the nightly live music acts and disco sessions, recorded concerts are shown on a big screen.

🚩 F6 ✉ Rua do Escondidinho, Carvoeiro 🕐 Daily 7pm–4am

KATEDRAL

Locals from Portimão mingle happily with holidaymakers at this

---

THE RIGHT KIT

Don't worry if you arrive in the Algarve without sports equipment; golf courses, tennis courts and water sport complexes can all provide the right equipment for hire by the day or week.

huge and very popular disco, perched like a giant cube on the cliff top. There's a downstairs bar, but things really happen upstairs, where a light show accompanies the latest dance sounds.
➕ F6 ✉ Avenida Tomás Cabreira, Praia da Rocha ☎ 282 414 557

ON THE ROCKS

Catch the last rays of the sun on the terrace before heading inside this modern dance bar. Expect loud music, dancing to live bands on Fridays and occasional soccer on the giant TV.
➕ F6 ✉ Avenida Tomás Cabreira, Praia da Rocha ☎ 282 416 144

VALE DA PINTA GOLF

A beautiful clubhouse, bowling green, spa and pool are on offer at this golf resort, set in undulating landscape near Carvoeiro. The Championship course winds past well-positioned bunkers and two lakes. Maximum handicaps of 27 for men and 35 for ladies are required.
➕ F6 ✉ Pestana Golf and Resorts, Carvoeiro ☎ 282 340 900

VALE DE MILHO GOLF

www.pestanagolf.com
A great course for inexperienced golfers with just 9 holes. It's set on the outskirts of Carvoeiro, where the terrain is up and down to say the least and offers experienced golfers the chance to brush up their short game. No handicap is required.
➕ F6 ✉ Vale de Milho, Carvoeiro ☎ 282 358 502

Restaurants

PRICES

Prices are approximate, based on a 3-course meal for one person.
€€€   over €60
€€   €25–€60
€   under €25

ABABUJA (€€–€€€)

www.ababuja.com
On the river front, Ababuja's dining room spills outside in summer to the open-air grill, where the chefs turn out dozens of plates of super-fresh sardines. The accent is on fish, with the day's catch served grilled, or as a *caldeirada* (mixed fish stew) or *massada de* *peixe* (mixed fish cooked with pasta and scented with coriander). Desserts are good, with chocolate tart, flambéed figs and a delicate mango mousse all on the menu.
➕ E6 ✉ Rua da Ribeira 11, Alvor ☎ 282 458 979
🕐 Daily lunch and dinner

SARDINES

Grilled sardines are synonymous with the Algarve and you'll find charcoal grills everywhere with chefs preparing plate after plate. They're at their best in the summer, and are cooked with the heads on and rarely gutted or scaled.

CASA VELHA (€€)

This big, bustling restaurant may be firmly aimed at tourists, but it's none the worse for that, and beautifully situated in the heart of historic Silves. Seafood, shellfish and fish are the specialties, with everything fresh from the coast or stored in the seawater tanks in the dining room. Choose from the bewildering variety of shellfish, or pick out a spider crab, sea urchins or a lobster for a real treat; cheaper options include sardines and chicken.
➕ G5 ✉ Rua 25 de Abril, Silves ☎ 282 445 491
🕐 Daily lunch and dinner

CERVEJARIA PRAIA DA ROCHA (€)

Definitely a cut above many of the other budget restaurants in Praia da Rocha, this friendly, bustling *cervejaria* is packed with locals—always a good sign. Enjoy a drink and a snack or tuck into one of the excellent value daily specials or the grilled meats and fish.

➕ F6 ✉ Edifício Colunas, Praia da Rocha ☎ 282 416 541 🕐 Daily lunch and dinner

JARDIM DAS OLIVEIRAS (€€)

www.jardimdasoliveiras.com
Mountain food is the order of the day in this farmhouse restaurant on the road between Monchique and Foia. Set in an olive grove, the restaurant has a pleasant terrace and there are cosy fires inside for cooler evenings. The food is spot-on, making full use of local specialties, such as cured and fresh meats and cheeses, roast meat, hearty stews and delicious vegetables dishes such as beans with rice and carrots and cabbage stew. A great change from all that fish.

➕ E3 ✉ Sítio do Porto Seco, Monchique ☎ 282 912 874 🕐 Daily lunch and dinner

LA MONA LISA (€€)

Italian owned, Italian run, with wood-fired pizza ovens imported from Italy, this is the place to come if pizza's your thing. The freshly made dough is rolled thin and piled high with a huge variety of toppings—other simple Italian dishes are also on offer, and don't miss the garlic bread.

➕ F6 ✉ Vale Centianes, Carvoeiro ☎ 282 358 724 🕐 Daily lunch and dinner

PARAÍSO DO MONTANHA (€€)

Sitting on the terrace here is mountain paradise indeed, with sweeping views down to the coast and fresh hill air. Run by the same family for over 30 years, the restaurant serves unpretentious, high-quality local food—start with a plate of *presunto* (smoked mountain ham), then move onto casseroled rabbit or charcoal-grilled lamb or steak, before indulging that sweet tooth with Dom Rodrigo—a rich egg and almond dessert, an Algarve specialty.

➕ E3 ✉ Estrada da Foia, Monchique ☎ 282 912 150 🕐 Daily lunch and dinner

SUESTE (€€€)

Ferragudo is noted for its fish restaurants and this is the pick of the bunch, beautifully situated at the end of the fishermen's quay, with fabulous sunset views across the River Arade. Eat whatever's off the boats that day, grilled to perfection over charcoal and served with simple boiled potatoes and a salad—quintessential Algarvian food. No reservations so arrive early to avoid waiting.

➕ F6 ✉ Rua da Ribeira 91, Ferragudo ☎ 282 461 592 🕐 Daily lunch and dinner

U VENÂNCIO (€)

www.uvenancio.com
You can't come to Portimão and not sample the famous grilled sardines beside the river, and this smart little restaurant is the best of the inexpensive fish restaurants that line the waterside. A plate of sardines, a chunk of bread, a mouthful of salad, all washed down with a light *vinho verde*—the true taste of the Algarve.

➕ F6 ✉ Zona Riberinha Entre-Pontes 4, Portimão ☎ 282 423 379 🕐 Daily 12–11

COUVERT

As you sit down, every restaurant waiter in the Algarve will bring you a basket of bread and a plate of spreads—butter, sardine paste and cheese are the most common, together, perhaps, with a few olives, some marinated vegetables and slices of *chouriço*. This is the *couvert*; eat as much or little as you like, and the cost will be added to your bill. It makes a good starter in view of the hugely generous portions served in Portugal.

The eastern central Algarve stretches from lively Albufeira in the east, to the gentler delights of Faro and the Ria Formosa in the west. Between is a varied coast, with golf courses and beaches, while inland the Barrocal is home to charming towns and villages set in lovely upland country.

Tavilhão

Ameixial

Vascanito

Medronheira

Portela

Barrigões

545
Miradouro
do Caldeirão

Cerro de
Alganduro

Vale da Rosa

Cabaça

474
Negros

Salir

Palmeiros

Corcitos

Vicentes   Querença

Aldeia
de Tor   396

C A L

Clarianes

Assumadas

396

Loulé   270

Corotelo

Fonte da
Murta

Bordeira

Goncinha

Benatrite

Poço da
Amoreira

Santa Bárbara
de Nexe

IP1

Esteval

Milreu

Imancil

**Igreja Capela de
São Lourenço
dos Matos**

Estói

2   2,6

Pechão

Braciais

Conceição

**Quinta
do Lago**

Vergilios

Faro   **Faro:
Cidade Velha**

Faro ✈

L   M   N

Albufeira

HIGHLIGHTS

● The views from the Igreja de Santana terrace
● Rua Candida dos Reis, with its buzz, craft stalls and pavement bars
● The cliff walk to the coves west of town

TIPS

● A toy train connects Albufeira with Montechoro, 9am–1am (Jun–Sep until 4am).
● In August, don't miss the Festa da Ourada, in honour of the fisherman's saint.

Combining 21st-century tourist essentials with the vestiges of the fishing village it once was makes Albufeira a holiday town par excellence. Beaches and cliffs, bars and restaurants, nightclubs and shops, and hotels to suit every pocket are all here, tucked into the narrow, steep streets of the old town and spreading out into the new development to either side.

The Old Town To see the last traces of pre-1960s Albufeira, head for the eastern Fisherman's Beach, where boats are still pulled up on the sand, before exploring the whitewashed maze of narrow cobbled streets that form the Old Town, perched high above the main beach. The focus of this miraculous survivor is the main square, the Largo Engenheiro Pacheco, a broad space ringed with

Clockwise from left: A narrow, cobbled street in the Old Town; the long and golden sandy beach; a view up to the Old Town from the beach; fishing boats pulled up on the sand; the parish church in the Old Town

popular bars. From here, Rua 5 de Outobro leads to a tunnel blasted through the cliff to give access down on to the beach. At low tide you can walk its full length, using the lift at the west end or the escalator at the east to bring you back up.

Away from the Beach For culture, you can check out the Museo Arqueológico (Praca da Republica, Oct–May Tue–Sun 10.30–4.30; Jun–Sep Tue–Sun 2.30–8; free), with local finds and some great photos of old Albufeira, or visit the main churches, the Ermide de São Sebastão and the Igreja de Santana, both mainly 18th-century. Further out, new Albufeira sprawls in all directions. West is the marina, hop-off point for boat trips; to the east lies Montechoro, known as The Strip, a lively and quintessential package tour resort with a great beach and buzzing nightlife.

THE BASICS

✚ H6
🍴 Huge range of restaurants, bars and cafés
🚌 Bus terminal is 2km (1.2 miles) from the middle of town; shuttle bus to town
🚆 Ferreiras (6km/3.7 miles)
♿ Few
🛈 Rua 5 de Outobro, tel 289 585 279; Jul–Sep Tue–Thu 9.30 –7, Fri–Sun 9.30–1 and 2–5.30; Oct–Jun Mon–Fri 9.30–1 and 2–5.30

Alte

Left to right: the parish church; the Fonte Grande*; water cascading from a spring*

THE BASICS

➕ J4

🍴 Restaurants and cafés in village

❓ Day trips run to Alte from the major coastal resorts. Nearby: the Barrocal (▷ 82), Paderne (▷ 80) and Salir (▷ 83)

ℹ️ Estrada da Ponte 17, tel 289 478 666; Mon–Fri 9–12.30, 2–5.30

DID YOU KNOW?

● Manueline architecture gets its name from Dom Manuel, who reigned from 1495–1521. This style of architecture is a mix of Moorish and Spanish with a Portuguese twist, featuring maritime motifs like ropes, rigging and anchors.

It may not have great sights or museums and it's miles from a beach, but the white village of Alte, deep in the limestone hills of the Barrocal, pulls in the crowds with charm alone.

Through the Village Winding cobbled streets wend their way through Alte, a picture-postcard village spread across a hillside. Its architecture is Algarve vernacular at its best—filigree chimney pots, dazzling white low-roofed houses, their façades picked out in blue, ochre and green, and gardens brimming with vibrant flowers. A half-hour or so meandering through the warren of little streets is time well spent. Start at either end of the village and walk through, pausing to take in Alte's one sight, the beautiful 16th-century Igreja Matriz (Mon–Sat 8–1, 3–7). Near the top of the village, it's fronted by a terrace, where benches are placed beneath the carob trees. The main portal is richly carved with knotted rope decoration, a fine example of the unique Portuguese style known as Manueline, while the interior has a glittering altarpiece and tiles of heavenly blue.

A Stroll to the Fontes Outside town, to the east, footpaths lead to a couple of natural springs (*fontes*), where locals flock for Sunday barbecues and picnics. Follow the signs to *Fonte Pequena* (Little Spring), where there's a restaurant housed in the old mill, or walk further to the *Fonte Grande* (Big Spring), a less-manicured spring further up the reedy valley, where there are picnic tables and bars in the shade beside a weir.

Estói

Pretty tiles on the terraces (left) and a water feature (right) at the Palácio de Estói

For years, the sleeping beauty of a palace known as the Palácio do Visconde de Estói slumbered in this inland town. It has now been restored as a *pousada* and the overgrown gardens are being replanted.

The Palace and its Gardens The sugar-pink Palácio de Estói, the only palace in the Algarve, dates from the 19th century, when the Conde de Cavalhal constructed a miniature version of the royal Rococo palace of Queluz near Lisbon. After his death, it was eventually bought by the family of Estói. For years, both the palace and its surrounding gardens gently crumbled; the house was shuttered, while the gardens were overgrown. In spring 2009, after being immaculately refurbished, the palace opened to guests as a very classy hotel. Inside, the great hall has become a dining room and the old kitchens, with their lovely 19th-century tiles, have been transformed into a bar. There is a pool and swanky bedrooms and suites. The São José Chapel, with its beautiful altar and pulpit decorated in gold leaf and celestial imagery, is still used for religious ceremonies. The approach avenue, lined with palm and orange trees, still gives access to the original double stairway, decorated with tiles and statuary, which leads up to the reflecting pool and terrace in front of the palace.

Estói Village The village itself is worth a quick look, particularly the Igreja Matriz on the main square; it was built after the 1755 earthquake and designed by Fabri, who also worked in Faro.

THE BASICS

✚ M6
❓ Nearby: the Roman ruins at Milreu (▷ 82)

Pousada
www.pousadas.pt
✉ Palácio de Estói, Estói
☎ 289 990 150

HIGHLIGHTS

● The São José chapel
● The *azulejos* on the terrace steps
● The garden

Faro: Cidade Velha

TOP
25

Set within a circle of walls, Faro's Cidade Velha (Old Town) encapsulates the town's 16th-century golden age. Cobbled streets and spacious and elegant squares are the backdrop for a splendid cathedral and the Algarve's oldest museum.

Largo da Sé Walk from the harbour through the Arco da Vila, a beautiful 19th-century neoclassical arch, designed by the Italian Fabri, and head uphill to the Largo da Sé (Cathedral Square). Lined with orange trees, it's the perfect setting for the Sé itself, the stately Paço Episcopal (Bishop's Palace), and the old town hall, a long range of pleasingly rational buildings. The Sé (Jul–Aug Mon–Sat 10–6, Sep–Jun 10–12.30, 1.30–5; inexpensive) is a squat mix of Gothic, Renaissance and baroque elements, first constructed in the 13th and 14th

An elegant row of houses in Faro's Old Town (left); the bell tower of Faro cathedral (middle); visitors strolling through the cobbled streets of the Old Town (right)

centuries. It needed a rebuild after the Earl of Essex sacked it in 1596, and another after the earthquake of 1755. The interior has some beautifully tiled side chapels and a red and gilt organ. Take the outside stairs to reach the clock tower and its huge views over the town and lagoon.

Convento de Nossa Senhora da Assunção

This serene 16th-century convent houses the Museu Municipal de Faro, a well-presented collection of local finds spanning the centuries, whose chief treasure is a fine 4th-century Roman mosaic paving of Neptune, unearthed a few hundred metres from here. The museum's rooms open off a lovely cloister, all light airiness and balanced proportions. Other exhibits include Roman statues, Moorish lamps and potteries and an eclectic and provincial collection of paintings.

THE BASICS

🞢 b5
🛈 Rua da Misericórdia 8–12, tel 289 803 604; May–Sep Mon–Fri 9.30–7, Sat, Sun 9.30–1, 2–5.30; Oct–Apr Tue–Thu 9.30–5.30, Fri–Mon 9.30–1, 2–5.30

Museu Municipal de Faro
🞢 b5
✉ Largo Afonso III, 14
☎ 289 897 400
🕔 Oct–May Tue–Fri 10–6, Sat–Sun 10.30–5; Jun–Sep Tue–Fri 10–7, Sat–Sun 11.30–6 (last admittance 30 min before closing)
♿ Few
💶 Inexpensive

Igreja Capela de São Lourenço dos Matos

TOP
25

HIGHLIGHTS

● The cupola
● The high altar
● The scenes at the bottom of the main panels showing fishing and hunting
● The architectural details depicted in tiles

TIP

● It's worth popping into the Centro Cutural São Lourenço below the church, to admire the sculpture garden and take in one of the art exhibitions shown here.

Walk into the interior of this modestly-sized church, and you'll be surrounded by deepest, clearest blue and glittering gold. Every wall and floor surface is tiled with hand-painted *azulejos*, while the ceiling and altar are richly gilded.

The Church Decoration There's been a church here for centuries, but today's little gem probably dates from the mid-16th century, surviving the 1755 earthquake. In 1730, was adorned with tiles by the master craftsman, Policarpo de Oliveira Bernardes. Legend says the work was commissioned by northern aristocracy, down in the Algarve for some hunting; at any rate, such a decorational scheme would have been expensive. The tiles were designed specifically to complement the church's architecture—the *trompe l'oeil*

Beautiful azulejos (left) decorate the stunning interior of the church (right); detail of a painting (bottom left) on the pretty whitewashed exterior of the church (bottom right)

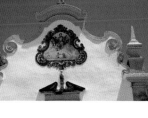

cupola is particularly stunning—and probably made near Lisbon and shipped by boat to the Algarve for installation. Every tile was individually painted from drawings by the artist, glazed and fired and then reassembled in the church like a giant jigsaw.

The Story of St. Lawrence The tiles tell the life story of St. Lawrence, the church's patron saint, a Roman patrician who was martyred in AD258. The narrative starts on the wall to the right of the altar and unfolds in a clockwise direction with a series of panels showing the saint renouncing his wealth and performing miracles. Things get more exciting on the left-hand wall, where the panels depict the saint's death. Legend states that he was roasted on a gridiron, only interrupting his constant prayer to ask his torturers to turn him as he thought one side was sufficiently well cooked.

THE BASICS

➕ L6
✉ On N125 east of Almancil
🕐 Sep–end May Tue–Sat 10–1, 2.30–5, Sun, Mon 2.30–5; Jun–Aug Tue–Sun 10–1, 2.30–6, Mon 2.30–5
🍴 Café at Centre Cultural (€)
♿ Good
💰 Moderate

Loulé

DID YOU KNOW?

● Loulé is famed for its traditional crafts such as basketry, copper-beating and leather-working, all Moorish legacies and now, sadly, dying out. Try Rua da Barbacá, near the castle, to see what's left.

TIPS

● Parking can be difficult, so aim to arrive early on market days.
● Loulé's *Carnevale* (late February or early March) is one of the Algarve's best.

Loulé's cobbled lanes, Moorish castle ruins and Gothic church are a world away from the beach resorts. Discover a true Algarvian town, where prosperous Portuguese rub shoulders with peasants from the country at its Saturday market.

The Town Loulé is the Algarve's largest inland town, tumbling down a hillside that's rich in orange and lemon groves. The old town draws the crowds, but it's worth taking in the modern pedestrian-only streets and the broad boulevard that runs through the town to the historic core. Here you'll find the medieval castle, home to the Museu Municipal (Mon–Fri 9–5.30, Sat 10–2; inexpensive), featuring a few prehistoric, Roman and medieval relics. Climb the stairs to reach the old town walls from where there are views

Clockwise from top left: Nossa Senhora da Piedade; the bell-tower of the Igreja Matriz; a view over the red-tiled rooftops of Loulé; brassware for sale in a shop on Rua da Barbacá

down to the coast. Near here is the Igreja Matriz, rebuilt in the 16th and 18th centuries on the site of the mosque—the minaret was retained and now serves as the bell-tower. For a contrast, head uphill to the startling spaceship of a building that's Loulé's newest church, Nossa Senhora da Piedade.

The Markets Loulé's main attraction has always been its markets. Daily produce markets take place in the splendid Moorishly-inspired 1900s Mercado Municipal, where superb fresh fish, fruit and vegetables jostle for space with bread and sausage stalls, honey-sellers and peasants offering their own produce. On Saturdays it overflows into the surrounding streets, while on the town outskirts there's a huge gypsy market, where you'll find everything from clothes and shoes to pottery, kitchenware, baskets, and plants and flowers.

THE BASICS

➕ L6
🍴 Numerous bars and restaurants in town
🚌 Daily buses from Albufeira, Faro and Quarteira
❓ Nearby: São Lourenço at Amancil
ℹ️ Avenida 25 Abril 9, tel 289 463 900; May–Sep Mon–Sat 9.30–7; Oct–Apr Mon–Sat 9.30–5.30

Paderne

The village of Paderne (left); the ruins of Paderne Castle, built in the 12th century (right)

THE BASICS

➕ J5
🍴 Restaurants and cafés in town
🚌 Hourly buses from Albufeira
♿ Castle: none
💷 Castle: free
❓ Nearby: Alte (▷ 72)

DID YOU KNOW?

The Moors introduced:
● Irrigation, wheel wells and water mills
● Terracing for cultivation
● Oranges, lemons, peaches and loquats
● Almonds
● Rice
● Paper-making

TIP

● Wear flat, comfortable shoes if you're planning to walk out to the castle.

The Algarve gets its name from the Moorish al-Gharb, the name the Moors gave to their western independent kingdom in the ninth century, and the castle they built at Paderne brilliantly illustrates their power and engineering ability.

Power base Castelo de Paderne was built by the Moors in the 12th century, one of a series of fortresses they constructed in the Algarve to bolster their power away from their capital at Xelb (Silves, ▷ 56). The Christian monarchs won back most of Portugal from the Moors by the mid-12th century, but they hung on in the Algarve until 1249, when Afonso III finally took Faro. There was a major battle at Paderne as part of this push, and in 1249, Dom Paio Peres Correía, commanding the knights of the Order of Christ, Portugal's main military order, took the castle.

The Castle A bumpy track runs the 2km (1.2 miles) from the village of Paderne to the ruins of its grand castle. It's a lovely walk through olive groves and fields, with the motorway soaring overhead providing a sharp contrast to the tranquillity. Clamber up to the top to explore the ruins, with their huge crumbling walls, and enjoy great views over the countryside around. Look out, too, for the remains inside the fortress of the 14th-century Ermida de Nossa Senhora do Castelo, built to celebrate the return of the Christian faith. Walk back along the river to the village, where the only sight is the Igreja Matriz (1506); it's a pleasant place to soak up some sun and the relaxed atmosphere.

Vilamoura

Vilamoura marina at dusk (left); Roman remains at the Museu Cerra de Vila (right)

Vilamoura, one of the largest purpose-built leisure complexes in Europe, offers holidaymakers all they could conceivably want. Come here to play golf, go fishing, take a boat trip, eat and drink, enjoy the beach and visit the casino.

What to Do Vilamoura's focus is the 1,000-berth marina; well-designed, crammed with sleek yachts and high-speed leisure craft, and surrounded by high-rise hotels, bars and restaurants. A network of over 200km (124 miles) of roads links the hub with the hotels and the numerous villas that nestle in beautifully maintained sub-tropical planting. This hinterland is also home to Vilamoura's six golf courses. The expensive Old Course and the Vila Sol are the tops, but the Pinhal, Laguna, Millennium and Oceânico are challenging too, with fairways lined with pines and plenty of water hazards. From the marina boats run along the coast, offering sightseeing, dolphin watching, big-game fishing, jetskiing and parascending.

Beaches and Walking Vilamoura has two beaches, the Praia da Marina to the east, with over 3km (1.9 miles) of fine, Blue Flag sand, and the Praia de Falésia to the west of the marina, reached by a footbridge over an inlet. If you enjoy walking, strike out on one of the cliff-top trails that fan out from the resort. You can also explore the Museu Arqueológico do Cerro da Vila, an archaeological site with fascinating traces of its Roman, Visigothic and Moorish inhabitants—the on-site museum will explain it all.

THE BASICS

✚ K6
🍽 Numerous restaurants, bars and cafés
🚌 Buses from Albufeira, Faro and Quarteira
❓ Six golf courses. Big-game fishing trips. Nearby: Quarteira (▷ 82), Almancil, Vale do Lobo and Quinta do Lago (▷ 83)

Museu Arqueológico do Cerro da Vila

✉ Av. Cerro da Vila
☎ 289 312 153
🕐 May–Oct daily 9.30–12.30, 2–6; Nov–Apr daily 9.30–12.30, 2–5
 Inexpensive

DID YOU KNOW?

● The world-record black marlin, weighing 743kg (1,634 lbs), is claimed to have been caught off Vilamoura.
● The Algarve has three casinos—one at Vilamoura and the others at Monte Gordo, near Tavira, and Praia da Rocha.

More to See

BARROCAL

The Barrocal area, named after the limestone that underlies it, covers around a quarter of the Algarve and stretches right over the east. The central section runs over the gentle hills north of Loulé, a fertile farming landscape which produces vegetables, citrus fruit, almonds, figs and carobs. It's a world away from the coast and a good area to explore for a change of pace—you can explore villages like Alte (▷ 72) and Salir (▷ 83), or enjoy a walk in the hills; tourist offices have details.

🔁 K5

MILREU

www.ippar.pt

Visiting the Roman villa of Milreu, while needing a bit of imagination, gives a good chance to appreciate how important the fertile Algarve was to the Empire. This patrician's villa was inhabited from the 2nd to the 6th centuries, with changes made to the layout over the years. Today's ruins nestle round a peristyle

villa—you can still see traces of the central patio and its 22 columns—and the apse of a nearby temple. This was built in the fourth century and dedicated to the water gods; it was later converted into a Christian basilica, making it one of Portugal's earliest churches. The site's chief draw are the mosaics, all with a fishy theme; you'll find them in the peristyle and on the walls of the ruins of the baths.

🔁 M6 ✉ Estói ☎ 289 997 823 🕐 Apr–Sep Tue–Sun 9.30–12.30, 2–6; Oct–Mar Tue–Sun 9.30–12.30, 2–5 🍴 No café or bar 🚻 Few 💶 Moderate

QUARTEIRA

Once purely a fishing town, Quarteira still sends its boats out daily and you can admire the catch, along with fruit and vegetables, at the splendid market held daily right by the fishing harbour. From here, a long sandy beach, wonderfully safe for small children, stretches east towards Vilamoura. It's backed at the far end by a wide promenade, planted with

A mosaic detail at the Roman villa of Milreu

The Barrocal area provides a great habitat for wildlife

palms, while behind loom the tower blocks that went up when the town was developed for tourism in the early 1970s. It's a cheap, cheerful and very Portuguese holiday town, an attractive contrast to the glitz of the surrounding resorts.

➕ K7 🛈 Praça do Mar, tel 289 389 209; May–Sep daily 9.30–7; Oct–Apr daily 9.30–5.30

SALIR

If you're visiting Alte, you'll probably pass through Salir, a little-known and beautifully sited farming village set on a hilltop in the midst of rolling countryside. The Moors settled here, and the vestiges of their castle, just a few walls and a ruined turret, still remain. Stroll out through the village to see the remains before wandering uphill, past the whitewashed houses, to the Igreja Matriz (open for servies only) and its little square. This is overshadowed by the town water tower, home to an incredible number of swifts and swallows.

➕ L4

VALE DO LOBO AND QUINTA DO LAGO

www.valedolobo.com
www.quintadolago.com

The up-market enclaves of Vale do Lobo and Quinta do Lago are golf and leisure resorts built for serious money, where sumptuous villas and hotels lie in sub-tropical gardens and sports facilities are second to none. Don't let the exclusivity put you off; both places are worth a look. Each has superb golf courses and huge beaches: stretches of soft, clean sand that are ideal for children. Quinta do Lago's beach is reached by a wooden bridge crossing the Ria Formosa and dunes; there are a couple of nice nature trails with excellent bird-watching running from here round the eastern end of the Parque Natural da Ria Formosa (▷ 94). At Vale do Lobo, which has won a Green Globe award for environmental awareness, you can hire beach loungers and umbrellas and enjoy the superb beach in the sort of comfort only money can buy.

➕ K7 (Vale do Lobo); L7 (Quinta do Lago)

The hilltop village of Salir

Horse-riding is just one of the many activities on offer at Quinta do Lago

A Walk around Faro

There's more to Faro than its Old Town. Stroll round the harbour, main shopping streets, an off-beat museum and two churches.

DISTANCE: 2km (1.2 miles)   **ALLOW:** 45 minutes walking; 2.5 hours with visits

START

ARCO DA VILA
✚ a4

END

HARBOUR
✚ a3

1 With your back to the Arco da Vila, turn left and walk along to the end of the range of buildings. Cross the street diagonally left to the entrance of the Centro Ciência Viva museum.

2 Leave the museum and cross the road to the water's edge, following the water round until you are level with the shady town garden, the Jardim Manuel Bivar. Walk through this to the far end, cross the road, and turn right into Rua Francisco Gomes, closed to traffic and one of Faro's main shopping streets.

3 Branch right at the junction and continue into Rua Santo António, taking the right-hand turn down Rua Pinheiro Chagas to reach the Museu Regional do Algarve, an enjoyable collection of local crafts and some fascinating old photographs.

6 Backtrack to São Pedro and walk down the right-hand side of the church and into Rua da Madelena. Cross the square at the end and take Travessa da Madelena to the Avenida da República. Turn left and walk along to the harbour area.

5 Bear left from here into the Largo do Carmo, dominated by the church of the same name. Walk through the church garden to visit the Capela dos Ossos, a macabre little chapel whose walls are decorated with human bones.

4 Leave the museum and retrace your steps, this time crossing Santo António diagonally left to walk down Rua Vasco da Gama. At the bottom, bear left into Rua José Estevão to reach the church of São Pedro, a lovely 16th-century church with a spectacular gilded altar.

Shopping

ARTYS

There's a good selection of books and stationery here, including a wide range of publications—some in English—about the Algarve, many beautifully illustrated.

➕ b3 ✉ Rua Santo António 10, Faro ☎ 289 878 314

CENTRO DE ARTESANATO

Although Loulé's tradition of craft making is sadly disappearing, there's a good selection of its famous handicrafts on offer here. You can choose from decorative pottery, baskets, mats made from palm leaves or cork, woodcarving, copperwork, leather and hand-woven rugs.

➕ L6 ✉ Rua da Barbaca 11/13, Loulé

FORUM ALGARVE

www.forumalgarve.net
Possibly the Algarve's best shopping mall, with a giant supermarket, fast-food outlets and a multiplex cinema. It is well laid out, with a central courtyard and fountain, and branches of Massimo Dutti, Zara, Cortefiel and Lacoste among the many shops.

➕ Off map at a2 ✉ On N125 at west end of Faro ☎ 289 889 300 🕐 10am–11pm (midnight in summer)

GRIFFIN BOOKSHOP

www.griffinbookshop.com
The Algarve's best English-language bookshop stocks plenty of local guide books, illustrated gift books and relaxing holiday reading. They have a wide selection of paperbacks, including lots of well-priced second-hand books.

➕ L6 ✉ Rua 5 de Outobro 206-A, Almancil ☎ 289 393 904

LA LOJAS

Anyone who finds themselves short of accessories will find a good selection of shoes, bags and jewellery here.

➕ H6 ✉ Rua Cândido dos Reis 20/22, Albufeira ☎ 289 513 168

LOULÉ MARKET

The best produce market in the Algarve, with stalls selling fish, shellfish, fruit and vegetables,

country sausages, ham and cheese, local honey and herbs and spices. Stock up here for piri-piri ingredients or browse for take-home food souvenirs and gifts.

➕ L6 ✉ Praça da República, Loulé 🕐 8–12

MUNDO DO SAPATO

www.shoeworldshop.com
One of several Algarve branches of this discount shoe warehouse, where good-quality Portuguese footwear is on offer as well as brand names such as Nike, Shark, Ecco and Adidas.

➕ H6 ✉ Retail Park–Loja B, Tavagueira, Albufeira ☎ 289 585 485

QUINTA DO LAGO SHOPPING

Just outside the Quinta do Lago estate, this big shopping complex has a wide range of shops, bars and restaurants. You'll find branches of Max Mara, Ralph Lauren, Victor Victoria, Richard menswear and La Perla, as well as excellent cosmetic stores, newsagents and plenty of gift shops.

➕ L7 ✉ Quinta do Lago ☎ 289 392 027

TRAKINAS-LOJA

Grannies should head here to source adorable and practical baby and children's wear from international and Portuguese designers.

➕ c3 ✉ Rua Santo António 10, Faro ☎ 289 878 818

Entertainment and Activities

AQUASHOW

www.aquashowpark.com
The best waterpark in this area, with slides, loops, tunnels, Europe's biggest water rollercoaster, Portugal's biggest wave pool, a toddler's play area and snack bars.
🏁 K6 ✉ Just off N125 at Quatro Estrados, near Quarteira ☎ 289 389 396 🕐 Jun, beginning to mid-Sep 10–6; Jul 10–6.30; Aug 10–7

CASINO VILAMOURA

www.solverde.pt
Vilamoura's casino has over 500 slot machines, and table games including Black Jack, roulette and poker. The smart casual casino stages regular floorshows, and has a restaurant, bars and a disco. Take your passport as proof of age if you want to gamble.
🏁 K6 ✉ Quarteira ☎ 289 310 000 🕐 Generally daily 4pm–3am, but check website as times vary

CENTRO CIÊNCIA VIVA

www.ccvalg.pt
This hands-on science complex is a great place for kids to learn about the natural world, with a particular emphasis on the sea. There are interactive games, fish and sea life and enthusiastic multilingual staff to bring it to life.
🏁 a5 ✉ Rua Comandante Francisco Manuel, Faro ☎ 289 890 920 🕐 Jun to mid-Sep Tue–Sun 10–8; mid-Sep to May Tue–Fri 10–5, Sat–Sun 11–6

GOLF

www.valedolobo.com
www.quintadolago.com
The three developments of Vilamoura, Quinta do Lago and Vale do Lobo have a total of 11 golf courses between them. Green fees and conditions vary but most expect a handicap certificate and play isn't cheap. Clubs and electric caddies are for hire at all courses.
🏁 K6–L7

KADOC

www.kadoc.pt
Kadoc is one of the Algarve's coolest clubs, and it's certainly the biggest, pulling in more than 1,500 partygoers who come here to dance all night to sounds chosen by international DJs.
🏁 H6 ✉ Estrada da Vilamoura, Albufeira ☎ 917 812 315 🕐 Jun–Jul Sat–Sun 11.30pm–6am; Aug daily 11.30pm–6am; Sep–May only for Carnaval and festivals

KIDS IN THE ALGARVE

Beaches can be dangerous and small children will be happiest on the gently shelving sandy beaches in the east, where the tides are less hazardous. Look out for inflatable rides, such as ringos and bananas, which are potentially lethal for smaller children. Watch out, too, for the strength of the sun and keep children covered up and in the shade during the middle of day.

KISS

The best bet for all-night partying in the Albufeira area, with five bars and two dance floors, and guest DJs throughout the summer. You'll find it at the southern end of Montechoro.
🏁 H6 ✉ Rua Vasco da Gama, Areias de São João, Albufeira 🕐 May–Sep daily 11–6; Oct–Apr Sat, Sun 11–6

PARQUE DES CIDADES

www.parquecidades-eim.pt
The Algarve's main stadium was built for Euro 2004 and provides a well-equipped and stunning venue for sporting events and big-name concerts in southern Portugal. The 30,000-seat stadium hosts a Summer Festival in June, with international bands and groups.
🏁 L6 ✉ Loulé ☎ 289 893 201

ZOOMARINE

www.zoomarine.com
A day out here is a highlight for many families. This is a park that combines swimming pools and funfair rides with an aquarium and animal and bird enclosures, and there are shows throughout the day. The site has fast-food restaurants and a water slide.
🏁 H6 ✉ Estrada Nacional, Guia, Albufeira ☎ 289 560 300 🕐 Mid-Mar to mid-Jun, 2nd week Sep–Oct daily 10–6; mid-Jun to 1st week Sep daily 10–7.30

Restaurants

PRICES

Prices are approximate, based on a 3-course meal for one person.

€€€   over €60
€€   €25–€60
€   under €25

A RUINA (€€–€€€)

www.restaurante-ruina.com
Albufeira's highest profile beachside restaurant offers dining on four storeys with summer eating on the beach or roof terrace and two levels inside. The fish couldn't be fresher, and it's simply and beautifully cooked, but bear in mind that it's priced by weight and shellfish will practically break the bank—ask to see your selection weighed before it's cooked.
➕ H6 ✉ Praia dos Pescadores, Largo Cais Herculano, Albufeira ☎ 289 512 094 ⏰ Daily lunch and dinner

A TASKA (€€)

Just near the Largo do Carmo you'll find this excellent restaurant, where locals tuck into generous portions of regional dishes such as bean rice with fish, fried squid and grilled fish. There are two dining rooms, one with an open fire for the windy winter months.
➕ b2 ✉ Rua Alportel 38, Faro ☎ 289 824 739 ⏰ Mon–Sat lunch and dinner

ADEGA NORTENHA (€€)

www.adeganortenha.pt
The decor here is simple, light and stylish, with a nice warm glow from the long, polished wood counter. There are satisfying dishes on the menu, including *cataplana* casserole (a mixture of seafood and pork), roast lamb and tuna steaks.
➕ b4 ✉ Rua Praca Ferreira de Almeida, Faro ☎ 289 822 709 ⏰ Daily 12–12

AFONSO III (€€)

This true community restaurant has been pleasing locals for years with its fresh fish, grilled meat and house specials such as *cataplanas* and *arroces*. Portions are huge, the house wine is good, but don't count on subdued lighting or romantic décor—this

FISHY DELIGHTS

You'll find a huge variety of fish in the Algarve, usually served plainly grilled. Many restaurants will expect you to choose from the chilled cabinet and will then cook your choice to order; prices on the menu are often per kilo and they will weigh your choice before it's cooked. Fish is often expensive, and shell fish more so, so, if you're watching the budget, go for *sardinhas* (sardines), cooked on a charcoal grill, a true taste of the Algarve.

is a great-value, everyday restaurant, family run with speedy and friendly service.
➕ L6 ✉ Praça Manuel Arriaga 32–33, Loulé ☎ 289 422 161 ⏰ Daily lunch and dinner

BICA VELHA (€€)

Tourists rub shoulders with locals at this popular restaurant, located in one of the oldest buildings in Loulé. Despite its inland position, the accent's on fish, served with a wide selection of vegetables and salads. Booking ahead is advised.
➕ L6 ✉ Rua Martim Moniz 17–19, Loulé ☎ 289 463 376 ⏰ Mon–Sat dinner

CHURRASQUEIRA A TENAZINHA (€)

Eat inside or outdoors at this friendly, family-run restaurant overlooking Quarteira's main street, and enjoy some of the best chicken piri-piri in the Algarve, as well as well-cooked fish and steaks. The salads are generous and the house wine slips down a treat. They also do chicken to take away. The restaurant offers superb value for money.
➕ K7 ✉ Avenida Doutor Francisco, Sá Carneiro, Bloco A, Quarteira ☎ 289 388 066 ⏰ Daily lunch and dinner

COFFEE ALIANÇA (€)

This Faro institution, with its dimly lit, wood-panelled interior and

traditional menu, is a local favourite. It's one of Portugal's oldest establishments, founded in 1908, and it retains its old atmosphere. You can enjoy salads, omelettes and a range of sandwiches either inside or outdoors. 🚇 a3 ✉ Praça Francisco Gomes 25, Faro ☎ 289 801 621 🕐 Daily 8am–10pm

FUZIO'S (€€)

There are two pretty terraces in the garden of this Mediterranean restaurant where Italy is the main inspiration. The menu includes staples such as *insalata tricolore* (mozzarella, tomatoes and basil) and pasta is made on the spot; meat and fish are well-sourced. This is an attractive and up-market restaurant that's ideal for a leisurely dinner. 🚇 K7 ✉ Rua do Comércio, 286, Almancil ☎ 289 399 019 🕐 Thu–Tue dinner

IZZY'S RESTAURANT AND BEACH BAR (€€–€€€)

www.izzysbeachbar.com
There's nothing between you and the ocean as you eat at Izzy's. Children are provided with a playground and their own menu. Enjoy a *caipirinha* or *mojito* before choosing from the long menu, where the accent's on fish. Prawns are a specialty and you can choose from the fish counter or simply settle for a home-

made burger. It's also a good place for Sunday lunch, when there's live music. 🚇 L6 ✉ Vale do Garrão, Almancil ☎ 289 396 984 🕐 Daily lunch and dinner

O REI DOS FRANGOS (€)

A good bet in Albufeira that serves up mouth-watering charcoal-grilled chicken—not for nothing does its name mean King of the Chooks—with pungent piri-piri, as well as tasty grilled *bife* (steak) and a good *cataplana*. There are few frills but it offers great value. 🚇 H6 ✉ Travessa dos Telheiros 4, Albufeira ☎ 289 512 981 🕐 Daily lunch and dinner

O ZUCO (€)

Tucked away off the main square, this simple restaurant packs in the

---

THE FULL MONTY

All main dishes in Portugal are automatically served with a selection of potatoes and seasonal vegetables and often a small side salad as well, so there's no need to order extra veg. Chips and/or rice are served with meat and boiled potatoes with fish—if you want chips, ask when you're ordering. Portions are very big, and it's quite acceptable to ask for a half serving.

---

locals who come here to feast on down-to-earth grills and superb shellfish. You can eat at tables or the bar and sample specialties such as *porco alentejana* (pork with clams from the Alentejo), *cozida* (stew with chick peas) or the *pratos do dia* (daily special). It really is excellent value all round. 🚇 H6 ✉ Travessa do Malpique 7, Albufeira ☎ 289 588 768 🕐 Thu–Tue lunch and dinner

WILLIES (€€€)

www.willies-restaurante.com
For a big night out, head for the Michelin-starred Willies, where you'll find excellent food served with style in elegant surroundings. The restaurant is in a quiet residential area near the beautiful Pinhal golf course, a lovely setting that truly comes into its own in the evenings. The tables are beautifully set and the atmospheric lighting, flowers and flickering candles add to the ambiance. The service is professional and discreet. Choose from dishes ranging from light as a feather seafood ravioli to delicate sea bass, and perhaps round it all off with lemon cream and berries served in a sugar basket. Booking ahead is advised. 🚇 K6 ✉ Rua do Brazil 2, Vilamoura ☎ 289 380 849 🕐 Thu–Tue dinner

Eastern Algarve

The eastern Algarve coast has huge sandy beaches and marshy lagoons, its towns vary from salty ports to 18th-century elegance and its sheltered waters are protected as a natural park. Inland, rolling hills stretch north and to the east is the lovely river valley of the Guadiana.

Monte Vascão   Puerto de
                la Laja
Santa
Marta   Afonso Vicente

Farelos   Coito

Cerro da Vinha

        Pereiro
Marim
                    Alcoutim
caria   Alcaria   273
  a   Fornalha   124

              Fonte
              Zambujo   Balurco
                        de Baixo

        Palmeira
Alcaria   Guerreiros
Queimada   Soudes   do Rio
Zambujal   Corte de   Corte das
              São Tomé   Donas
Preguiças   Furnazinhas   Vale de
                          Pinheiro   Tenência   Laranjeiras
    Odeleite
        Fortes   Barragem
                de Odeleite

Várzea   Monte de   Odeleite   Alcaria
        Baixo Grande

Cabaços   Estrada
                Corte
  Cume   Beliche   do Gago
                Alcarias
        Cortelha   Barragem   Azinhal
Beliche   de Beliche
do Cerro
        Vale de Ebros   Cerro
                      do Anho   Junqueira
Alcaria   Carrapateira

              Ribeiro   Monte Francisco
Estorninhos   229   **Castro
              Miguel Anes   Marim**
Ribeira da Gafa   Montinho
Zimbral   **Vila Real
              São Bartolomeu   de Santo
              Altura   António**
ira da   A22   Coutada   Monte
Palma   Nora   Vila Nova   Gordo
São   de Cacela
Marcos
      Conceição   **Cacela
                  Velha**   Ponta da Areia
Tavira   Cabanas

            Golfo   de   Cádiz

Ilha de Tavira

                        0   5 km
                        0   3 miles

Q   R   S

E

122

122.1

124

IC27

E 01

122

125·1

125

9

Olhão

A decorative balcony (left); the harbour (right); a view from the church tower (opposite)

TOP
25

THE BASICS

- N7
- Restaurants, bars and cafés
- Buses from Faro and Tavira
- Rua dos Combatentes da Grande Guerra
- Few
- Ferries to Culatra; time-tables from tourist office or from ticket office (on quayside)
- Nearby: Parque Natural da Ria Formosa (▷ 94)
- Largo Sebastião Martins Mestre 8A, tel 289 713 936; May–Sep Mon–Fri 9.30–12.30, 2–6; Oct–Apr Mon–Fri 9.30–1, 2–5.30

DID YOU KNOW?

● When you dig in to the sardine paste served at the start of a meal in virtu-ally every restaurant in the Algarve, it's likely that it was made at Olhão; the commer-cial harbour is ringed with enterprises pertaining to all things concerning fishing.

Salty, workaday Olhão stretches back in a Moorish-style warren of narrow streets behind its waterfront, from where regular ferries run to the delightfully laid-back island of Culatra, home to fishermen and the perfect spot for relaxed summer days.

The Town Olhão is a down-to-earth working port, the biggest fishing hub in the Algarve, with an outlying commercial harbour packed with serious trawlers. Once through this, in the heart of the old town, you're in for a treat. Shady gardens run beside the sea, flanked by the town's modern market buildings, one housing the vegetable, fruit, cheese and meat markets, the other entirely devoted to myriad varieties of seafood and fish (Mon–Fri 7–2, Sat 6.30–3). Cross the road to explore the old town proper, where narrow, cobbled streets are lined with cube-like, flat-roofed houses whose architecture bears witness to Olhão's strong trading links with Morocco. The main sights are the 18th-century Igreja Matriz, dedicated to Nossa Senhora do Rosário (Our Lady of the Rosary; daily 9–12, 3–6), and the Museu da Cidade (Tue–Fri 10–12.30, 2–5.30; Sat 10–1), an appealing jumble of archaeological finds, model fishing boats and old photographs.

The Islands Ferries run throughout the year to Culatra, a sandspit island across the lagoon, whose main settlement is Farol. Holiday homes and fish-ermen's huts overlook the water, and a lighthouse rises above the narrow paths that wind through the dunes to the fabulous beaches on the south side.

Parque Natural da Ria Formosa

TOP
25

HIGHLIGHTS

- The dunes and beaches
- The marshes and lagoon
- Wild flowers in spring
- Seabirds and waders

TIP

- Boats run year-round to the lagoon islands from Olhão (▷ 92), and from Faro from May to September.

The area enclosed by the boundaries of the Parque Natural da Ria Formosa is a truly special place—where a traditional way of life combines with an immensely rich natural habitat to create a little-known side of the Algarve.

The Park Stretching from outside western Faro to Manta Rota near the Spanish border, the Parque Natural da Ria Formosa is 47.6sq km (28.7sq miles) and was established in 1987 to protect the islands and lagoons that run along the east end of the Algarve. These lagoons, riddled with tidal flats, islets, channels and salt marshes, form a unique ecological environment and are important for birds. Resident, migratory and over-wintering birds all feed here, while the dunes and marshlands are rich in flora. Around 7,500 people live within the

The Parque Natural da Ria Formosa—home to tidal flats, channels, beaches, lagoons and salt marshes—attracts a wide variety of birdlife

park, most working in lagoon-related activities—nearly 80 per cent of Portuguese clams and other shellfish are reared here. In summer, the superb island beaches attract thousands, and the park authorities must balance environmental needs with the demands of tourism.

Learning More To help this, the Centro de Educação Ambiental de Marim (Environmental Education Centre) was set up near Olhão, where an area of coastal land and lagoon includes an example of virtually everything the park contains. Here you'll find an interpretative complex, salt pans, a traditional sea-water mill powered by the tides, woodland, dunes and a lagoon, on which an old tuna fishing boat sails. Don't miss the friendly group of Portuguese water dogs, a web-toed species bred for work with fishing boats.

THE BASICS

www.portal.icnb.pt
🔢 M7

Centro de Educação Ambiental de Marim
✉ Quinta do Marim, Quelfes, Olhão
☎ 289 700 210
🕐 Mon–Fri 9–5.30 (times may be extended; weekend opening under consideration–call to check)
♿ Good (access paths suitable for wheelchairs)
💶 Inexpensive

Rio Guadiana

TOP 25

HIGHLIGHTS

● Castro Marim (▷ 102)
● Foz de Odeleite
● Gueirreiros do Rio
● Alcoutim (▷ 102)

The beautiful river valley of the gently flowing Guadiana is dotted with villages and planted with orchards and vineyards. Drive to Alcoutim or take a boat to enjoy a relaxed day exploring another facet of the Algarve.

TIP

● Boat trips run from Vila Real either to Alcoutim or Foz de Odeleite, with swimming stops and lunch provided en route. Contact Rio-Terramar (tel 968 831 553; www.rotaminerio.de) or Riosul (tel 281 510 200; www.riosultravel.com).

A Few Facts From its mouth in the Atlantic the Rio Guadiana rises in the south-western Spanish province of Albacete and is roughly 800km (497 miles) long . It's only navigable for the last 68km (42 miles), from the Alentejo region, through the Algarve, and down to its mouth at Vila Real de Santo António; for the final 40km (25 miles) it forms the border that divides Portugal from Spain.

Along the River Heading north, Castro Marim (▷ 102) is the first settlement in the valley; from

here you can access the Reserva Natural do Sapal, an important wetland area along the river. There are trails through the marshlands, home to the extremely rare Mediterranean chameleon. Further on, the valley narrows as you approach a string of tiny settlements, the most important of which is Foz de Odeleite, set at the mouth of a tributary and surrounded by vineyards and fields of olive trees, oranges and vegetable patches. Look out for the communal bread ovens and the pumpkins and fruit drying on the flat-roofed houses. Further on, citrus trees and vineyards surround Guerreiros do Rio, where the tiny Museu do Rio (daily 9.30–1, 2.30–6; inexpensive) fills you in on river life and history—in Portuguese. From here it's another few miles to charming Alcoutim (▷ 102), a tranquil river port whose castle faces its Spanish rival across the water.

THE BASICS

✚ S4
🍴 Restaurants, bars and cafés in Castro Marim and Alcoutim
🚫 None
⛴ Ferry from Alcoutim to Sanlúcar de Guadiana (Spain)
🛈 Castro Marim: Rua Dr José Alves Moreira 2–4, tel 281 531 232; Mon–Fri 9.30–1, 2–5.30
🛈 Alcoutim: Rua 1 de Maio, tel 281 546 179; May–Sep Fri–Mon 9.30–12.30, 2–6, Tue–Thu 9.30–7; Oct–Apr Fri–Mon 9.30–1, 2–5.30, Tue–Thu 9.30–5.30

HIGHLIGHTS

- Igreja da Misericórdia
- Santa Maria do Castelo
- Palácio da Galeria contemporary exhibition complex
- Ponte Romana
- Quatro Aguas
- Ilha de Tavira

TIP

- You can hire a bike to explore the town and get to the beach.

Tranquil and homogenous, the lovely 18th-century town of Tavira, packed with churches and harmonious mansions, lies on the River Gilão, from where fishing and excursion boats head towards the Ilha de Tavira with its superb beach and warm sea.

The Town Three hundred years ago, Tavira, founded in Roman times, made its money from tuna fishing; the profits paid for the construction of the churches and solid houses that surround the elegant central Praça da República. This stands on the south bank of the river, here spanned by a 'Roman' bridge that's actually 17th-century, and leads to the narrow streets that are home to some of the town's best restaurants. From the *praça*, you can explore the heart of the town, a hilly

Clockwise from top left: A bridge spanning the River Gilão; a bell-tower and a clock tower rise above the rooftops; riverside house with a triple-gabled roof; decorated honeypots for sale at the market; salt pans; the exterior of a Manueline church

tangle of narrow streets and old houses that contrast with the broad riverside avenues. Tavira is rich in churches and convents; pick of the bunch are the beautiful Igreja da Misericórdia, built between 1541 and 1551 by Pilarté, a mason who worked at Belém near Lisbon, and Santa Maria do Castelo. The Moorish castle ruins, set in immaculate gardens, lie just up the hill, a good place for a pause, though you might prefer the riverside gardens and the old market and its cafés.

Out of Town From here, a toy train runs seawards to Quatros Aguas, the ferry departure point for the Ilha de Tavira, where there's a superb sandy beach, one of the best in the Algarve. Alternatively, head east across the River Gilão for Albacora, where a small museum tells the story of the tuna fishing industry.

THE BASICS

✛ P6

🍴 Restaurants, bars, cafés

🚌 Buses from Faro, Olhão and Vila Real

🚊 1km (0.6 miles) from middle of town

♿ Few

⛴ Ferry from Quatro Aguas to Ilha de Tavira

ℹ️ Rua da Galeria 9, tel 281 322 511; May–Sep Fri–Mon 9.30–1, 2–5.30, Tue–Thu 9.30–7; Oct–Apr Fri–Mon 9.30–1, 2–5.30, Tue–Thu 9.30–5.30

Vila Real de Santo António

HIGHLIGHTS

● Praça Marqûes de Pombal
● Museu Manuel Cabanas
● A river cruise
● Shopping

TIP

● If you head for Spain remember clocks are one hour ahead and, unlike the Portuguese, the Spanish take a long siesta.

For a taste of 18th-century rationalism combined with plenty of retail therapy, head for Vila Real de Santo António, situated on the banks of the River Guadiana opposite Spanish Ayamonte.

In Town Founded in 1773 to replace an earlier settlement swallowed up by waves and shifting sand, Vila Real was the brain-child of Portugal's chief minister, the dynamic Marqûes de Pombal, who applied the same design tenets he had used in the rebuilding of Lisbon's Baixa district. A grid design was drawn up, pre-cut stone shipped in and the entire town was virtually completed in six months. Arrow-straight streets of handsome buildings surround the central square, the Praça Marqûes de Pombal, with its orange trees, cafés, church, Câmara Municipal and former barracks.

Clockwise from top left: Relaxing in the main square, the Praça Marquês de Pombal; an 18th-century building with windows set into the tiled roof; a boat on the River Guadiana; the waterfront with the harbour in the distance

What to Do You could take in the Museu Manuel Cabanas (May–Oct Mon–Fri 10–1, 3–9; Nov–Apr 10–1, 3–7; free), on Praça Marquês de Pombal, where you can see woodcuts and paintings of the Algarve in the 1950s by this local artist, or visit the Igreja Matriz, with its glowing stained-glass windows. Strolling the heart of the town and the riverbank is a pleasure, or you could hop on the ferry and enjoy a few hours in Spain across the River Guadiana, or take a river cruise. Boats run upriver from the waterfront, a lovely way to spend a sunny day. For many, Vila Real's shops are a major attraction, with northern European and Spanish shoppers looking for good buys in linens, woollen and cotton goods. For sea and sand, head for Monte Gordo, a big, clean resort with high-rise buildings, a casino and a great beach.

THE BASICS

🚏 S5

🍴 Restaurants, bars and cafés

🚌 Buses from Faro, Olhão and Tavira

🚉 Avenida da República

♿ Few

🚢 From the marina to Ayamonte, Spain, every 30 or 40 minutes, 9–8

❓ Nearby: Castro Marim and Monte Gordo (▷ 102)

ℹ Avenida Marginal, Monte Gordo, tel 281 544 495; Mon–Fri 9.30–1, 2–6

More to See

ALCOUTIM

This ancient river port, occupied by the Greeks, Romans and Moors, stands above the Guadiana, the ruins of its 14th-century castle evidence of its historic importance as the shipping hub for the copper from nearby São Domingos. You can visit the castle and its archaeological museum, then relax beside the river or take the ferry across the river to Sanlúcar in Spain.

🔢 R2 🍴 Restaurants, bars and cafés
🛈 Rua 1 de Maio, tel 281 546 179; May–Sep Fri–Mon 9.30–12.30, 2–6, Tue–Thu 9.30–7; Oct–Apr Fri–Mon 9.30–1, 2–5.30, Tue–Thu 9.30–5.30

CACELA VELHA

Cacela Velha, a whitewashed village perched on a bluff at the end of a road, is the Algarve as it used to be. It's little more than a handful of cottages, a church and an 18th-century fort, while below the village lies the lagoon and beach. Walk down through the dunes and olive trees to wade out to the barrier island at low tide.

🔢 Q6 🍴 Restaurant and cafés

CASTRO MARIM

Two castles bear witness to the past strategic importance of Castro Marim, a little village overlooking the marsh-lands of the River Guadiana. The main castle, incorporating an earlier 13th-century Moorish fortification, was built in 1319 as the headquarters of the Order of Christ; the walls, with their great views, went up in the 1800s and are topped with ramparts. Across the town are the remnants of the 17th-century fort of São Sebastião.

🔢 S5 ♿ None 🛈 Rua Dr José Alves Moreira 2–4, tel 281 531 232; Mon–Fri 9.30–1, 2–5.30

SÃO BRÁS DE ALPORTEL

The main draw here is the appealing Museu do Trajo (Mon–Fri 10–1, 2–5, Sat, Sun 2–5; inexpensive), packed with traditional costumes and agricultural artefacts. The old heart of the town has a fine Igreja Matriz and the delightful Jardim da Verbena, with an open-air swimming pool.

🔢 M6 🛈 Largo S Sebastão 23, tel 289 843 165; Mon–Fri 9.30–1, 2–5.30

Pretty whitewashed buildings in the river port of Alcoutim

The Reserva Natural do Sapal, with the town and castle of Castro Marim in the distance

A Drive up the Guadiana River Valley

A drive through a river valley and its villages, and back to the coast through the hills of the Serra de Alcaria, little touched by tourism.

DISTANCE: 122km (75.8 miles) **ALLOW:** 2.5 hours; with stops 4–5 hours

START

CASTRO MARIM
➕ S5

❶ Head north from Castro Marim on the N122 (signed Beja/Mertola). Leave this road at Odeleite (18km/11 miles) and follow the Castro Marim signs through the village. Turn right to Alcaria (also signed Foz de Odeleite) at the T-junction and follow this road, turning left to Foz de Odeleite.

❷ Look out for two landmark white castellated towers on your right, after which the road drops down to the River Guadiana. Go through Foz and continue beside the river.

❸ At Alamo the road swings briefly away from the river. Follow the signs at the mini-roundabout towards Alcoutim to rejoin the Guadiana at Guerreiros do Rio.

❹ A few kilometres further, past the *miradouro*, with its views of the castle of Sanlúcar de Guadiana, you can visit the remains of the Villa Romana do Montinho das Naranjeiras.

END

TAVIRA
➕ P6

❽ Branch left onto the N397, a beautiful road that twists and turns through high mountainous country, gradually descending to Tavira (40km/25 miles).

❼ Follow the N124 to Martim Longo. The road then swings south into increasingly hilly countryside, with ranges of hills opening up in front of you. Continue on to Cachopo (13km/8 miles).

❻ Leave Alcoutim on the N124, signposted Martim Longo. The road climbs to sparsely populated, rolling plateau countryside, with fields of superb wild flowers in late winter and spring.

❺ Continue on to Alcoutim.

Shopping

ATLÂNTIDA SPORTSWEAR

Spaniards flock across the border to shop at Vila Real so you'll find keen prices at this well-stocked store. There's a good selection of trainers, tops and work-out clothes, as well as sports accessories of all sorts. Brands include Billabong, Rip Curl, Reebok, Hi-Tec, Colombia and Salomon.
➕ S5 ✉ Rua 5 Outubro 27, Vila Real de Santo António ☎ 281 511 496

CASA DAS MALHAS

This traditional shop is the ideal browsing place for linens, wools, embroidery articles, haberdashery and souvenirs.
➕ P6 ✉ Rua José Pires Padinha 60–62, Tavira ☎ 281 322 514

CASA DO ARTESANATO DE TAVIRA

This is among the best of Tavira's craft shops, with examples of almost every type of local handicraft. You can buy miniature boats, hand-woven textiles and linens and baskets of every size, as well as local ceramics and other souvenirs.
➕ P6 ✉ Calçada da Galeria 11, Tavira ☎ 281 381 265

LUZ VERDE

There are two Luz Verde shops on Vila Real's main shopping street, and ladies should head here for one of the best selections of women's clothing in the eastern Algarve. Tops, skirts, trousers and dresses are all a cut above the offerings in the surrounding stores.
➕ S5 ✉ Rua Teófilo Braga 34, Vila Real de Santo António ☎ 281 513 811

MENTOL

This gem of a shop in a tiny alleyway in old Tavira specializes in beautifully made ladies' shirts in all styles and every type of natural fabric. There are soft cottons, linen and draped knitwear, and they will make to measure.
➕ P6 ✉ Travessa D Brites 8, Tavira ☎ 281 325 786

MERCADO DA RIBEIRA

Tavira's old market building, right on the riverside gardens, has been converted into a space

---

TEXTILES

Portugal has a long tradition of textiles manufacture, and there are bargains galore on offer in the way of pure cotton sheets and bedlinen, towels and tablewear. Prices are low and quality good, though you may have to search to find designs that truly appeal. Other good buys in pure cotton include T-shirts, dresses, beach wraps and men's shirts and underwear. There are also lovely hand-woven textiles on offer in *artesanato* shops.

---

where you'll find a range of souvenir and craft shops as well as bars and cafés—a good place to browse for an hour or so.
➕ P6 ✉ Rua José Pires Padinha, Tavira

MERCADO MUNICIPAL

The best daily market in the eastern Algarve is housed in two purpose-built halls right on the waterfront. Come here to gaze at the myriad variety of seafood and fish, and shop for picnic ingredients at the fruit, vegetable, cheese and bakery stalls.
➕ N7 ✉ Avenida 5 de Outubro, Olhão

RIA SHOPPING

www.riashopping.pt
The Algarve's newest shopping centre is a three-storey mall with around 70 shops, plus plenty of eating options, a play area and a cinema.
➕ N7 ✉ Estrada Nacional 125, 100, Olhão ☎ 289 714 751

SOL DOURADA

There are dozens of shops selling household linens of every description in Vila Real, and this is about the best. You'll find everything from towels and sheets, to pretty table cloths, children's bedlinen and clothes, and lovely bedcovers and quilts.
➕ S5 ✉ Rua Teófilo Braga 18, Vila Real de Santo António ☎ 281 543 527

Entertainment and Activities

AQUATAXIS
You'll need to take a boat across the lagoon to get to the best beaches around Tavira, and this company has a taxi and regular service from town or Quatro Aguas out to the Ilha de Tavira. Pick it up at the quay at Tavira to avoid the mile-long hike down to Quatro Aguas.
🔟 P6 ☎ 964 515 073
🕐 Sep–Jun 8–6, Jul–Aug 24 hours a day

CAMINHOS DA NATUREZA
www.caminhosdanatureza.pt
You can rent bicycles all over the Algarve, but for something a bit special Nature Paths are the answer. They run guided off-road biking into the lovely country behind the coast as part of a range of sporting activities, including hiking and trekking.
🔟 P6 ✉ Praçeta Marcelino Galhardo, Lote 6, Tavira
☎ 962 543 288

CASINO MONTE GORDO
www.solverde.pt
If you want a big night out, visit Monte Gordo, home to one of the Algarve's three casinos. There's a huge range of slot machines and games, and you'll find blackjack, poker and roulette at the tables. Floor shows, a disco, cabaret and a cinema will also keep you amused.
🔟 S5 ✉ Avenida Marginal, Monte Gordo ☎ 281 530 800 🕐 Check website

MONTE REI GOLF
www.monte-rei.com
This beautiful course, dotted with pines and following the contours of the rolling landscape, was designed by Jack Nicklaus and offers challenging golf on a par 72 course, with plenty of bunkers and water hazards. The clubhouse has a bar and restaurant and you can hire both clubs and shoes, though you'll need a handicap certificate (men max. 24, women max. 32) to play.
🔟 R5 ✉ Monte Rei, Vila Nova de Cacela ☎ 281 950 960

QUINTA DE CIMA GOLF
www.quintadariagolf.com
A series of lakes, connected by a stream, runs through this beautifully designed, championship-style, par 72 course, considered both interesting and testing. You'll need a handicap certificate to play. Clubs, trolleys and buggies are all for hire, and there's a restaurant and snack bar.
🔟 R5 ✉ Quinta de Cima, Vila Nova de Cacela ☎ 281 950 580

RIOSUL
www.riosultravel.com
As well as cruises on the Guadiana (▷ 96), this company also offers jeep safaris exploring the remote hills behind the coast of the eastern Algarve. You can go on a full day excursion by combining a river cruise, which includes lunch, with a jeep safari. Reserve in advance.
🔟 S5 ✉ Rua Tristão Vaz Teixeira, 15c, Monte Gordo ☎ 281 510 200

SANTA LOUCURA
Tavira's old market, right by the river, is home to this lively music bar, a good bet for some late-night partying. There's a flat-screen TV, good sound system and the occasional live act.
🔟 P6 ✉ Mercado Municipla, Loja 3, Tavira ☎ 965 412 676

TAVIRA TENNIS CLUB
For a change of pace after a lazy beach day, you can head for Tavira's town tennis club.
🔟 P6 ✉ Rua Dr. Silvestre Falcão Lote 7, 1º Posterior, Tavira ☎ 281 321 535

PEACE OR PARTY?
The best clubs and nightclubs in the Algarve are, unsurprisingly, in the big resorts and main towns. So you'll have to balance staying somewhere really attractive against what will certainly be a dearth of nightlife. In such places, after dinner entertainment will be little more than a stroll, a drink and perhaps a bit of live music at the weekend. Bear in mind, though, that Portuguese bars, even in tiny places, can be great fun and packed with young locals.

Restaurants

PRICES

Prices are approximate, based on a 3-course meal for one person.

€€€	over €60
€€	€25–€60
€	under €25

AQUASUL (€)

Tables spill outside from this pretty, mosaic-decorated restaurant where the Italian-inspired menu makes a welcome change from the Portuguese diet of fish and grills. Choose from light and leafy salads, a good range of pasta, or go for one of the thin and crispy pizzas from the wood-fired oven.
🚇 P6 ✉ Rua Dr A. Silva Carvalho, 13, Tavira ☎ 281 325 166 🕓 Tue–Sat dinner

ARENILHA (€–€€)

Brick arches and *azulejos* give a traditional feeling at this restaurant. In summer, there are tables outside where you can enjoy the usual range of Algarve dishes—fish, seafood and grills, with some good specials often featuring *bacalhão* (dried salt cod).
🚇 S5 ✉ Rua Almirante Cândido dos Reis, Vila Real de Santo António ☎ 281 544 038 🕓 Daily lunch and dinner

MALWA (€)

Portugal's historic links with India are reflected in this welcoming restaurant which specializes in Goanese cooking and curries. Fish and prawns are highly spiced and there's a selection of hot vindaloos, as well as milder kormas.
🚇 N7 ✉ Rua Vasco da Gama 2, Olhão ☎ 289 715 276 🕓 Daily lunch and dinner

O CORAÇÃO DA CIDADE (€–€€)

www.coracaodacidade.com
Come here at any time of day or in the evening to enjoy a drink, snack or full meal. The tables outside are a good place to watch the crowds and have an ice-cream or sticky cake, sandwiches and snacks at lunch or a plate of fish or grilled meat in the evening. Unpretentious and excellent value.
🚇 S5 ✉ Rua Dr Teófilo

RIVER VALLEY SPECIALS

The valley of the River Guadiana is the perfect place to sample specialties such as eels, either grilled over charcoal or stewed long and slow with tomatoes and garlic, and lamprey, an eel-like sucker fish, cooked with herbs, white wine and spices such as ginger. Local vegetable gardens in this fertile valley provide broad beans and peas in abundance, as well as salad vegetables; in summer, look out for *gaspacho*, a soupy tomato stew, similar to Spanish *gazpacho*.

Braga 19, Vila Real de Santo António ☎ 281 543 303 🕓 Daily 8am–11pm

O SOEIRO (€–€€)

This quintessentially Portuguese restaurant is humming at lunch, as tourists join locals to enjoy big plates of hearty, home-cooked food. Specials include eels, lamprey and mullet from the River Guadiana, country stews and game. Meat and chicken are cooked on the outside barbecue in summer. Wine comes in a jug and waiters are kept busy running up the hill to the tables set on the cobbles overlooking the river—a great find.
🚇 R2 ✉ Rua do Município 4, Alcoutim ☎ 281 546 241 🕓 Mon–Fri lunch; café Mon–Fri 9am–11pm

QUATRO AGUAS (€€)

This renowned restaurant is situated beside the water where the ferry leaves for the Ilha de Tavira. Tables are scattered beneath shady pines and umbrellas, so you can take in the wonderful views and birdlife as you sample dishes such as the superb *cataplana mar rico*, stuffed with prawns and other shellfish. The service is excellent and there is a comprehensive wine list.
🚇 P6 ✉ Quatro Aguas, Tavira ☎ 281 325 329 🕓 Tue–Sun lunch and dinner

There's more accommodation choice in the Algarve than anywhere else in Portugal. With options ranging from world-class luxury hotels to simple village rooms, you're guaranteed to find something to fit the bill.

Where to Stay

Introduction

The Algarve's hot tourist spots are those with the most accommodation choice, with resorts such as Albufeira, Vilamoura and Praia da Rocha topping the bill. These are ideal for a beach holiday, though you could also head for Carvoeiro, Lagos and Praia da Luz for something a bit smaller. If money's no object, consider a sumptuous villa at Vale do Lobo or Quinta do Lago, or check in at one of the Algarve's *pousadas*, beautiful hotels housed in historic buildings. Visitors who prefer to stay in rural surroundings should head west, or inland into the hills.

What to Expect

Portugal's hotels are graded between one and five stars, the rating reflecting their facilities, comfort and service. *Pensões* and *residências* are another option and are classified on a scale of one to three stars; the main official difference between them is that *residências* only provide breakfast, and sometimes not even that. The Algarve has a huge selection of self-catering accommodation. *Apartamentos* are normally available as weekly lets, as are villas, which can be wonderful, often having lovely gardens, their own pool and a daily maid service. These can be booked via specialist villa tour operators or direct with the owners (▷ below). If you're touring and want self-catering, *aparthotels*, serviced apartments in a complex or single building that can be rented on a daily or weekly basis, are the answer. You'll get the best value by either booking a package, or putting your own holiday together online. Rates throughout the Algarve can drop by 50 per cent or more during the winter.

BOOKING ONLINE

Most Algarve accommodation has its own website and their online rates offer considerable savings. Alternatively, you could book through reputable internet sites such as www.laterooms.com, www.expedia.com or www.lastminute.com. If you're looking for self-catering, try www.holiday-rentals.co.uk; they have over 2,000 Algarve properties.

The Algarve has a wide range of accommodation, including luxurious hotels and self-catering apartments

Budget Hotels

BALTUM

www.hotelbaltum.pt
Just 50m (55 yards) from the beach, and set on a lively, pedestrian-only street, this excellent-value hotel offers good-sized rooms with air conditioning, many with balconies. The multilingual staff are friendly and efficient and the hotel has its own restaurant and dining terrace. 51 rooms, 6 suites.
🔁 H6 ✉ Avenida 25 de Abril, Albufeira ☎ 289 589 102/3/ 🕐 Open all year 🚌 Buses to Faro and Portimão

CASA GRANDE

www.nexus-pt.com/casagrande
Casa Grande is a rambling old estate house, furnished with antiques and traditional pieces, its bedrooms painted in pastels, with high stuccoed ceilings. Staying here, and eating breakfast round the communal table, feels like enjoying a sojourn at a private house. The adjoining winery is now a restaurant. 9 rooms.
🔁 D6 ✉ Burgau, Lagos ☎ 282 697 416 🕐 Open all year 🚌 Buses to Lagos

ESTALAGEM ABRIGO DA MONTANHA

http://abrigodamontanha.com
Set high above Monchique on the road to Foia's summit, this granite-built inn is surrounded by a garden packed with camellias and citrus trees. Inside, stone walls, wood panelling and pretty fabrics are the keynotes. Rooms are good, the restaurant is excellent, there's a pool and terrace and cosy log fires in winter. 11 rooms, 3 suites.
🔁 E3 ✉ Corte Pereiro, Monchique ☎ 282 912 131 🕐 Open all year

NAVIGATOR

www.hotel-navigator.com
Perched on the cliff above the sea and beach, this *aparthotel* offers apartments with a double bedroom, bathroom, living room and well-equipped kitchen; all balconies have a sea view. The hotel has a pool and restaurant if you don't want to cook. 55 rooms.
🔁 A7 ✉ Rua Infante Dom Henrique, Sagres ☎ 282 624 354 🕐 Open all year 🚌 Buses to Lagos and Portimão

PENSÃO MIRAMAR

For good value in a genuinely Portuguese resort head for this clean and welcoming guesthouse in Quarteira. Set just back from the beach, it has good-sized rooms, all with bathrooms, TV and balconies. Some have sea views. Watch the sunset from the rooftop terrace. 23 rooms.
🔁 K7 ✉ Rua Gonçalho Velho 8, Quarteira ☎ 289 315 225 🕐 Open all year 🚌 Buses from Faro, Almancil and Vilamoura

PENSÃO TIVOLI FARO

www.pension-tivoli.net
For budget visitors this is a good find in Faro, though it can be noisy. Room standards are mixed; some have showers and balconies, all are high-ceilinged. There's a communal kitchen and a pretty roof terrace. No credit cards. 15 rooms.
🔁 b4 ✉ Praça Alexandre Herculano 6, Faro ☎ 289 829 825 🕐 Open all year

RESIDENCIAL LAGÔAS

Very popular with budget visitors, this well-known *pensão*, right near the historic heart of lovely Tavira, is easily recognizable by its black and white façade. Rooms are clean and more than adequate. No air conditioning; no credit cards. 12 rooms.
🔁 P6 ✉ Rua Almirante Cândido dos Reis 24, Tavira ☎ 281 322 252 🕐 Open all year 🚌 Buses to Faro

Mid-Range Hotels

PRICES

Expect to pay between €80 and €180 per night for two in a mid-range room.

BOA VISTA
www.hotelboavista.pt
The view is indeed beautiful from this hotel perched above Albufeira. All the varied and well-equipped rooms have sea views, and there are more from the terrace and pool, where a café serves drinks and snacks. The fifth-floor terrace restaurant is elegantly spacious with more great views and there's a spa. 84 rooms.
➕ H6 ✉ Rua Samorra Barros 20, Albufeira ☎ 289 589 175 🕐 Open all year

CARVOEIRO SOL
www.thecarvoeirosol.com
Set right beside the tiny beach at Carvoeiro, this modern and very comfortable hotel has its own pool and superb views from the front-facing rooms. The theme throughout is blue, white and clear yellow, public areas are open and comfortable and the big bedrooms have touches such as tea-making facilities. Rates drop dramatically in winter. 54 rooms.
➕ F6 ✉ Praia do Carvoeiro, Lagoa ☎ 282 357 301 🕐 Open all year

CASA BELA MOURA
Just 1km (0.6 miles) from the beach of Nossa Senhora da Rocha, this beguiling little hotel, set in pretty gardens with a pool, has traditionally furnished rooms with plenty of space. The style has Moorish touches, staff are professional and the breakfast will set you up for the day. 14 rooms.
➕ G6 ✉ Estrada de Porches, Alporchinhos, Porches ☎ 282 313 422 🕐 Closed Nov to mid-Feb

COLINA DOS MOUROS
There are superb views across the River Arade to historic Silves and its Moorish castle from this modern and very comfortable hotel. Facilities are good, with spacious bedrooms, a restaurant, bar and well-designed gardens, where you'll find the terrace and two pools. Ask for a room facing the river. 57 rooms.
➕ G5 ✉ Pocinho Santo, Silves ☎ 282 440 420 🕐 Open all year

SELF-CATERING AGENTS

Algarve self-catering specialists include Truly Algarve (0870 250 9841; www.villa-in-algarve.co.uk); The Real Algarve (0115 966 3661; www.therealalgarve.com), and, for visitors from the US, VillasInternational (800 221 2260; www.villasintl.com). All have a good range of varied accommodation and on-the-spot representatives.

ESTALAGEM DO GUADIANA
www.grupofbarata.com
There's a beautiful river view from the terrace and many of the bedrooms of this tranquil hotel, set on the River Guadiana. The perfect place to relax in peace, the hotel's pretty rooms all have terraces, there's a pool and a fine restaurant serving regional cuisine. 31 rooms.
➕ R2 ✉ Bairro do Rossio, Alcoutim ☎ 281 540 120 🕐 Open all year

ESTALAGEM DOM LOURENÇO
www.monchiquetermas.com
If you want to stay in the beautiful woodland that surrounds the thermal springs of Monchique, this pretty hotel is the pick of the bunch. The rooms are Portuguese in style, with wooden floors and some nice antique pieces, and the restaurant is excellent. The staff can arrange spa treatments for guests; these are scheduled for the mornings, leaving the rest of the day free. 12 rooms.
➕ F4 ✉ Caldas de Monchique ☎ 282 910 910 🕐 Open all year

FARO
www.hotelfaro.pt
Far and away the best choice in Faro, this sleek and comfortable hotel stands in the heart of Faro, and has great views over the harbour, the town and the lagoon

and its islands. Bedrooms are state-of-the-art, with minimalist bathrooms, and there's a superb rooftop terrace. The hotel has a restaurant and underground parking. 90 rooms.

⊞ a3 ✉ Praça D Francisco Gomes 2, Faro ☎ 289 830 830 ◷ Open all year

LOULÉ JARDIM

www.loulejardimhotel.com
You'd pay a lot more on the coast for a hotel of this category, making this pretty hotel, with its white and yellow exterior and spacious bedrooms, extremely good value. Ask for one of the fourth-floor rooms, which all have balconies. Other amenities include a rooftop pool, two bars and a terrace. 52 rooms.

⊞ L6 ✉ Praça Manuel de Arriaga, Loulé ☎ 289 413 094 ◷ Open all year

MONTECHORO

www.hotelmontechoro.pt
This vast resort hotel, set on Albufeira's outskirts and within easy reach of the liveliest bars, is a great choice for families. Facilities include two bars, a restaurant, a roof-top grill room, two pools, tennis courts, spa and live entertainment every evening. 322 rooms, 40 suites.

⊞ H6 ✉ Rua Alexandre O'Neill, Montechoro, Albufeira ☎ 289 589 423 ◷ Open all year 🚌 Courtesy bus to town and beach

PENSÃO RESIDENCIAL CANTINHO DA RIA FORMOSA

www.cantinhoriaformosa.com
This idyllic guest house is a taste of the Algarve as it used to be, a blue and white traditional building on a country lane, just a short stroll from the beach. Rooms are plain but comfortable, breakfast a treat. Horses are everywhere and they specialize in riding holidays. Book in advance, and bear in mind a car makes sense here. 8 rooms.

⊞ P6 ✉ Ribeiro de Junco, Vila Nova de Cacela ☎ 281 951 837 ◷ Open all year

RESIDENCIAL SALEMA

www.hotelsalema.com
This comfortable hotel overlooks the heart of this traditional fishing village and the beach. Rooms are air-conditioned and spotless; all have balconies. There's

A ROOM WITH A VIEW

The big, modern resort hotels are generally designed so that all bedrooms have a balcony where you can sit outside, but inevitably not all balconies have that coveted sea view. Specify if you want a view when you book and expect to pay a premium, which can be hefty in the peak months of July and August.

a bar and breakfast room, satellite TV and a truly Portuguese atmosphere. 32 rooms.

⊞ C6 ✉ Rua 28 de Janeiro, Praia da Salema, Budens ☎ 282 695 328 ◷ Open Easter–Nov 🚌 Buses to Lagos and Portimão

TIVOLI CARVOEIRO

www.tivolihotels.com
Literally built into the cliff face, this superbly equipped hotel, just outside Carvoeiro, is a good choice for families. The bedrooms are pretty; all have balconies and many overlook the sea. Facilities include an indoor pool, two outdoor pools, bars and restaurants, a health club, putting green and a dive outfit. Two rooms have been adapted for visitors with disabilities. Book online for the best rates. 289 rooms, 4 suites.

⊞ F6 ✉ Vale do Covo, Carvoeira ☎ 282 351 100 ◷ Open all year

TIVOLI LAGOS

www.tivolihotels.com
This resort hotel is an excellent choice for families. Set in the middle of town, and an easy stroll to the beach, the hotel has buffet and à la carte dining rooms, a bar, lounges, lovely gardens, an outdoor pool and another pool in the beauty spa. 313 rooms, 11 suites.

⊞ D6 ✉ Rua António Crisógono, Lagos ☎ 282 790 079 ◷ Open all year

Luxury Hotels

MEMMO BALEEIRA

www.memmohotels.com
This beautifully positioned cliff-top hotel, built in the 70s, has undergone a transformation to become the western Algarve's chicest boutique-style hotel. Bedrooms are sleek and minimalist. There are indoor and outdoor pools, a spa and one of the best hotel restaurants west of Albufeira. 105 rooms, 6 suites.

⊞ A7 ⊠ Vila de Sagres ☎ 282 624 212 ◔ Open all year ⊟ Buses to Lagos and Portimão

LE MÉRIDIEN PENINA

www.starwoodhotels.com
Set near the beach at Alvor, the Penina offers huge, comfortable rooms with superb bathrooms, four restaurants, mani-cured grounds, a spa and beauty salon, three golf courses, tennis, riding and impeccable service. 188 rooms and suites.

⊞ F6 ⊠ Penina, Apartado 146, Portimão ☎ 282 420 200 ◔ Open all year

MONTE DO CASAL

www.montedocasal.pt
Set in the hills just north of Faro, with wonderful views over lush gardens to the coast, this is one of the Algarve's most special hotels. Housed in an 18th-century villa and English-owned and run, this is a country-house hotel with a difference, where the accent is on luxury and exceptional service. Bedrooms all have their own terraces and the restaurant is Michelin rated. There are two pools and a beauty salon. 13 rooms, 6 suites.

⊞ M6 ⊠ Cerro do Lobo, Estoi ☎ 289 990 140/289 991 503 ◔ Open all year

QUINTA DO LAGO

www.hotelquintadolago.com
Generally acknowledged to be the Algarve's finest hotel of this size, this haven of calm is set by the sea in one of Europe's most luxurious golfing resorts. Beautiful gardens surround a hotel that has exquisitely decorated bedrooms, spacious public areas, the choice of Italian or Portuguese restaurants, three championship golf courses, tennis, riding, a pool and beauty salon. 121 rooms, 20 suites.

⊞ L7 ⊠ Quinta do Lago, Almancil ☎ 289 350 350 ◔ Open all year

SHERATON ALGARVE

www.sheratonalgarve.com
Set among pine trees and surrounded by the verdant green of its own golf course, the cliff-top Sheraton is a luxury hotel where children will be as welcome as their parents. Bedrooms are delightfully furnished with Portuguese decorative themes, there's a Moorish air to the bar and restaurant, and you can eat on the terrace overlooking the sea. 215 rooms.

⊞ H6 ⊠ Praia da Falésia, Apartado 644, Albufeira ☎ 289 500 100 ◔ Open all year

VILALARA

www.vilalararesort.com
This exclusive hotel, overlooking the sea and set in 12ha (30 acres) of breathtaking gardens, is one of Europe's foremost thalassotherapy (seawater treatment) centres, offering a full range of treatments to promote well-being and relaxation. There are five pools and two restaurants. 100 junior suites, 11 suites, 13 apartments.

⊞ G6 ⊠ Praia das Gaivotas, Alporchinhos, Porches ☎ 282 320 123 (reservations)/282 320 000 ◔ Open all year

Use these pages to plan your journey to the Algarve and to plan your travel once there. The Essential Facts give you everything else you need to know, and you'll also find a bit of historical background and a few basic language tips in this section.

Planning Ahead

When to Go

The Algarve has something for everyone all year. Winters are warmer than in the rest of Europe, though mid-October to December can be wet. Spring and autumn are the best times to come, as temperatures are ideal and things are not too busy. Summer can be extremely hot and very crowded.

TIME

L The Algarve is on the same time as the UK, and is 5 hours ahead of New York and 8 ahead of Los Angeles.

AVERAGE DAILY MAXIMUM TEMPERATURES

JAN	FEB	MAR	APR	MAY	JUN	JUL	AUG	SEP	OCT	NOV	DEC
59°F	61°F	64°F	70°F	75°F	86°F	95°F	99°F	91°F	82°F	66°F	63°F
15°C	16°C	18°C	21°C	24°C	30°C	35°C	37°C	33°C	28°C	19°C	17°C

Spring (mid–February to April) Spring is perhaps the best time to come, with sun and rising temperatures, and the countryside at its greenest and loveliest.
Summer (May–September) The ideal time for a beach holiday, though July and August temperatures are very high.
Autumn (October–November) October can still be very pleasant though expect rain by the end of the month and during November.
Winter (December–mid-February) Rain falls are high during December, but the temperature is pleasant; it can be very stormy and daylight hours are short.

WHAT'S ON

February *Carnival* (week preceding Shrove Tuesday): all over the Algarve; parades, bands and partying everywhere; the best at Loulé.
March/April *Holy Week*: processions in many towns, enacting scenes from the Passion of Christ.
Easter Sunday: processions.
April/May *FIA Rally of Portugal*: long weekend of motor sport along inland routes.
May *Atacar o Maio* ('attacking May'): on 1 May, with various folk festivals throughout the Algarve.
June *Algarve International Music Festival*: organized by Gulbenkian Foundation, with music and ballet at venues

throughout the region, runs until August.
Santos Populares: music, parades, food and drink in honour of Sts John, Anthony and Peter at towns throughout region.
July *Loulé International Jazz Festival*: local and international jazz musicians play concerts and jam around town every weekend.
Feira do Carmo: Faro, annual fair with handicrafts and entertainment.
August–September *Allgarve*: a series of classical and modern concerts and exhibitions across the region.
Silves Medieval Fair: markets and performers recreate

medieval life.
Fatacil Fair: Lagoa, agricultural trade fair.
Medieval Fair: Castro Marim.
Espectáculos de Folclore: folk festival, with acts from all over Portugal performing all around the region.
October–November *Feira de Santa Iria*: week-long fair in Faro.
São Martinho's day: marked with chestnuts and the first of the year's wine harvest.
December *Christmas Eve*: this is the main celebration, with a feast of *bacalhau* after Midnight Mass.
New Year's Eve: parades and fireworks through the Algarve.

Useful Websites

www.visitalgarve.pt
The Algarve's official website packs in the information, covering every aspect of every area of the region, with an excellent search engine and plenty of links. PDF brochures and leaflets to download, and full information on events.

www.algarvenet.com
Detailed site aimed at residents, visitors and the business community, with information on everything from tourist sites to travel, shopping, weather and sport. The information pages are particularly useful for advance planning.

www.thealgarve.net
Aimed at US visitors, this site offers a wealth of information on planning an Algarve vacation, with links to accommodation, car rental and golf booking, as well as information on the region's different municipalities.

www.visitportugal.com
The Portuguese Tourist Board's official site has a comprehensive Algarve section, with suggested itineraries, accommodation and other listings.

www.portugalvirtual.pt
Links with comprehensive hotel and villa listings, restaurant and bar listings, sport, shopping and transport tips.

www.albufeira.com
Aimed at visitors staying in and around Albufeira, this site carries detailed information on what's what and what's on in and around the town. Good links to accommodation, car rental, airport transport, restaurants, bars and clubs.

www.portugalresident.com
This website is popular with the British ex-pat community and has current news and background information on the Algarve in English, with a 'What's On' section that includes smaller, local activities.

PRIME TRAVEL SITES

www.bbc.co.uk/weather
Get five-day, accurate forecasts for the Algarve and much more.

www.travelmarket.com
Search and comparison site for flights, hotels and car hire.

www.fodors.com
A prime travel-planning site. You can research prices and weather, book air tickets, cars and rooms; ask questions from fellow travellers on the bulletin board and find links to other sites.

www.laterooms.com
Hotel room booking site, clearly laid out to allow comparisons, with some of the best deals on the web.

INTERNET CAFÉS

Net & News ✉ Edificio Bela Vista-lj 3, Albufeira ☎ 289 586 996 🕐 Mon–Sat 8.30–7.30, Sun 8.30am–1pm 💷 €2.80 per hour

João Palma Vieira ✉ Praceta Jaime Cortesão, Albufeira ☎ 289 543 314 🕐 Mon–Fri 10–8 💷 €1.50 per hour

Brito & Vasques ✉ Avenida Inf D Henrique, Edificio Verde Lago-lj, Monte Gordo ☎ 281 511 224 🕐 Tue–Sun 11–11 💷 Free with a drink

Getting There

ENTRY REQUIREMENTS

EU residents need a valid identity card which they must carry at all times; UK visitors need a passport. US, Canadian, Australian and NZ visitors need a passport valid for a further 6 months from the date of entry, and can stay for up to 90 days without a visa. Check for recent changes with the Portuguese embassy in your home country.

INSURANCE

EU nationals are entitled to medical treatment on production of the European emergency health card, but all visitors are advised to have private insurance that covers private medical treatment (including repatriation), baggage and money loss, accident compensation and personal liability. An annual policy is the best value; some UK private medical insurance will also cover you abroad. Keep all receipts in case you have to claim and report losses or theft to the police and obtain a written report; no insurers will consider your claim without this. Visitors from outside the EU must have medical insurance.

AIRPORTS

Faro international airport lies 6km (3.7 miles) west of the town. It has one terminal, which is served by scheduled, low-cost and charter airlines from all over Europe, and also handles internal Portuguese flights. Visitors arriving from outside Europe will have to fly in via Lisbon.

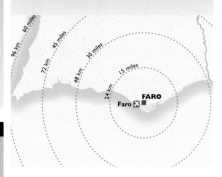

FROM FARO AIRPORT

To reach other parts of the Algarve from Faro airport (☎ 289 800 800; www.ana.pt; www.faroairportguide.com), you'll need to make the short trip to Faro's bus or train station, take a taxi, or book a private airport transfer or a seat on a shared shuttle bus. Private transfers will take you anywhere, while the shared shuttle bus serves the main resorts; both can be pre-booked at www.shuttledirect.com; the service leaves from outside the terminal building. Taxis, seating up to four people, will drive you anywhere in the Algarve. Buses 14 and 16 operate into Faro from 7am–9pm; the journey takes 20–25 minutes, tickets cost €1.65 and buses stop at the train and bus stations.

ARRIVING BY TRAIN

You can travel to the Algarve by train via Lisbon, which is accessible from the rest of Europe via Spain. International services to Lisbon either route through Burgos and Salamanca to reach Lisbon via Coimbra, or via Madrid and Marvão. From the UK, Eurostar (www.eurostar.com) runs to Paris, where you can pick up one of the

fast and frequent trains south (www.raileurope.co.uk). Journey times are long (29–35 hours from London to Faro) and fares are quite high compared with those of low-cost or charter flights; you will have to change trains several times en route.

ARRIVING BY BUS

International buses to Portugal from the UK are operated by Eurolines (☎ 08717 818181; www.eurolines.com), the foreign arm of National Express. Buses to Faro route through Lisbon; the journey time is approximately 38 hours and the adult fare around £210 one-way; under-12s and senior citizens travel half price.

ARRIVING BY CAR

Driving to Portugal takes time, and you might want to consider taking a ferry from the UK to Santander in northern Spain (Britanny Ferries ☎ 0871 244 0744; www.britanny-ferries.com). Driving from the UK, you can cross the Channel through the Channel Tunnel (Eurotunnel UK, ☎ 0870 535 3535; www.eurotunnel.com), then route through France and Spain. The best route runs south down the west coast of France on the E5, crossing the Spanish border at Irún, from where you head west across northern Spain on the A8 to Bilbao. Then take the E805 and the E80 into Portugal. From Guarda take the E806/A23 and pick up the A1-E01-E80 to Lisbon, continuing on the E01-A2 south to the Algarve. You should allow 48 hours driving time from London.

BUDGET AIRLINES

Budget airlines have frequent services to the Algarve from the UK.

Bmibaby (www.bmibaby.com) from Birmingham, Cardiff and East Midlands
Easyjet (www.easyjet.co.uk) from London, Glasgow, Belfast, Bristol, Newcastle, East Midlands and Liverpool
Flybe (www.flybe.com) from Exeter and Southampton
Jet2 (www.jet2.com) from Blackpool, Leeds and Manchester
Monarch (http://flights.monarch.co.uk) from London, Birmingham and Manchester
Ryanair (www.ryanair.co.uk) from London, Dublin, East Midlands, Shannon, Bournemouth and Glasgow
Thomas Cook (www.thomascookairlines.co.uk) from London Gatwick, Aberdeen, Belfast, Bristol, Cardiff, East Midlands, Leeds, Edinburgh, Glasgow, Humberside, Manchester, Newcastle and Birmingham

FARO AIRPORT

Faro airport has one terminal, and can be extremely busy, particularly during July and August, when check-in and baggage collection can be very slow. Services include banking, a tourist information desk, car rental desks, a self-service restaurant, snack bars and some shops.

NEED TO KNOW GETTING THERE

Getting Around

Megatur (www.megatur.pt) is the Algarve's main coach tour operator, offering a choice of dozens of day trips. They have a pick-up service from all the main resorts, running trips along the coast and into the hills to explore the villages, as well as evening dinner trips, and excursions to the theme and water parks, golf courses, shopping malls and the main towns of Faro, Albufeira, Portimão and Lagos.

BICYCLE AND MOPED HIRE

The 214km (133-mile) trans-Algarve cycle route runs from Cabo de São Vicente in the west to Vila Real in the east (www.ecoviasalgarve.org); it's a tough route and you may be happier simply renting a bike to get around your resort. Tourist offices have information on bike hire, or ask at your hotel. Bike hire is between €10–15 per day, while the cost of scooters and mopeds starts at around €30. The minimum age for renting scooters is 18 (over 23 for bikes over 125cc) and you must have held a licence for at least a year. Rental normally includes third-party insurance and helmet hire.

The main decision to make if you're visiting the Algarve is whether or not to hire a car. Many people come purely for the sun, sea and sand and will find that their chosen resort has everything they need for their holiday. If this is the case, and you just want the occasional day away from your base, a judicious mix of organized tours, public transport and taxis will be all you need. If you're visiting independently, and want to explore the region, touring from place to place, or simply want the flexibility your own transport gives, car hire is strongly recommended.

CAR HIRE
Car rental rates in Portugal are among the lowest in Europe and you'll find the best prices if you shop around and book in advance before you travel. All the major international hire companies have offices at or very near Faro airport and in the major resorts, and will collect you at the airport or deliver a car to your hotel or villa. Local firms offer slightly lower rates, but you may not be able to book in advance from home. Get round this by getting to your destination by taxi or public transport and then complete your car rental. This is a good method if you only want a car for a few days of your holiday. Check what insurance is included in the hire price, as you may well be pressured into buying extra cover when you pick up the car. You'll need your credit card as a deposit and to pay any additional charges. Bring the car back with a full tank to save money, no matter what the hirer promises. When driving, make sure you carry a photographic identity document (passport), which is mandatory at all times under Portuguese law.

BUSES
The Algarve is covered by a comprehensive network of buses run by the regional company EVA, as well as extra services supplied by some smaller operators. Tourist information offices and main bus stations (terminal rodoviário)

have route maps and timetables or go to
www.eva-bus.com. You can buy tickets at bus
stations or on the bus (have plenty of small
change). EVA sells a useful *passe turístico*, valid
for 3 days, which gives unlimited travel on all
routes for €25.50. Bear in mind that remoter
places and country areas have a limited bus
service.

TRAINS

CP (Caminhos de Ferro Portugueses ☎ 808
208 208; www.cp.pt) operates the Algarve line,
which runs the 130km (80 miles) from Vila
Real de Santo António in the east to Lagos in
the west. Trains are comfortable, cheap, scenic
and very slow, and you may have to change.
Bear in mind, too, that stations can be as far
as 4km (2.5 miles) from the town they serve.
You must buy a ticket before boarding; do this
on-line, at the ticket office or from machines in
stations. A one-way ticket is *ida*, a return *volta*.

FERRIES

There are ferries out to the sand bar islands in
the eastern Algarve; these run from Faro, Tavira
and Olhão during the summer months. The
international ferry between Portugal and Spain
runs across the River Guadiana between Vila
Real and Ayamonte in Spain every 40 minutes,
though most people now use the road bridge
upriver from Vila Real. There is an on-demand
ferry across the Guadiana from Alcoutim to
Sanlúcar in Spain.

GETTING AROUND YOUR RESORT

Albufeira is served by the
Giro bus service, operating 3
lines, with 105 stops, around
the city, outskirts and marina
areas from 7am–midnight
in summer, and 7am–10pm
between October and May.
One-day tickets cost €3,
single €1, 10-trip card €5.
Frequent *Vai e Vem* buses
link Portimão and Praia da
Rocha between 7.30am–
11.30pm, leaving from Largo
do Duque; tickets cost €1.80
single, €10 for a block of 10.

VISITORS WITH DISABILITIES

Facilities for visitors with
disabilities in the Algarve
still lag behind those in
northern Europe, though
the Portuguese will go out
of their way to make your
visit as easy as possible. Faro
airport has good facilities
and you can use the orange
European disabled car parking badge or the British blue
badge to park in disabled
parking spaces in the main
towns. New Generation
Tours offers various services
to visitors with disabilities,
including wheelchair rent-
als, airport transfers, taxi
services and excursions
(✉ Conceição de Faro Cx P
596, 8005-441 Faro
☎ 289 882 325/917 332
941; www.ngtours.com.pt).

Essential Facts

CONSULATES

UK ☎ 282 490 750
USA ☎ 217 273 300 (Lisbon)
Germany ☎ 289 803 181
Netherlands ☎ 289 820 903

MONEY

The official currency in Portugal is the euro (€). Banknotes come in denominations of 5, 10, 20, 50, 200 and 500 euros, and coins come in 1, 2, 5, 10, 20, 50 cent and 1 and 2 euro coins.

5 euros

10 euros

50 euros

100 euros

CUSTOMS REGULATIONS

● The limits for non-EU visitors are 200 cigarettes, 50 cigars or 250g of tobacco; 1 litre of spirits (over 22 per cent) or 2 litres of fortified wine (port), 2 litres of still wine; 50g of perfume. The guidelines for EU residents (for personal use) are 800 cigarettes, 1kg tobacco; 10 litres of spirits (over 22 per cent), 20 litres of fortified wine, 90 litres of wine, of which 60 can be sparkling, 110 litres beer.
● Visitors under 17 are not entitled to the tobacco and alcohol allowances.

ELECTRICITY

● The standard current is 220 volts AC.
● Plugs are round two-pin type. US visitors will need an adaptor and transformer.

HEALTH

● If you need a doctor or dentist, ask at your hotel as a first step; you are entitled to see a doctor on production of a European emergency health card. If you have medical insurance, most private doctors, many of whom are non-Portuguese, will come to your hotel.
● Pharmacies *(farmácias)* are open 9–1 and 3–7 Monday–Friday and 9–1 on Saturday. Every pharmacy displays in the window the address of the nearest 24-hour *farmácia*, which operate on a rota.
● Take prescription drugs with you and note the pharmaceutical name of your prescription as trade names may differ in the Algarve if you need a new prescription.

MONEY

● Credit cards are accepted all over the Algarve, though not normally for small purchases and in some smaller establishments.
● You can obtain cash from a cash machine (ATM), called *multibanco*, using your debit or credit card.
● You can change travellers' cheques at banks and *câmbios* (exchange bureaux) in larger towns and resorts.

NEWSPAPERS

● News-stands and kiosks in Algarve resorts have a large range of English-language newspapers and magazines. UK daily papers are generally on sale from about 11.30am.

● *The Euro Weekly News*, *The Portugal News*, *The Algarve Resident* and *Essential Algarve* magazine are English-language newspapers published locally, which have local news, listings and a satellite TV guide.

OPENING HOURS

● Banks: Monday–Friday 8.30–3.

● Shops: Monday–Friday 9–1 and 3–7; Saturday 9–1. Shopping malls open 7 days a week from 10–10 (midnight in summer). Large supermarkets are open from 9–10pm.

● Bars: 8.30–10pm or later.

● Restaurants: 12–3 and 7–10. In the main resorts many are open from 8–midnight.

● Post Offices: Monday–Friday 9–6.

TELEPHONES AND INTERNET ACCESS

● Public telephones *(credifones*, marked *comunicações)* take cards available from kiosks, tobacconists and post offices. Follow the instructions in the kiosk using the following international dialling codes: UK 00 44, USA/Canada 00 1, Irish Republic 00 353, Germany 00 49. The international code for calling Portugal is +351. Mobile phone reception is good throughout the Algarve.

● Public buildings, shopping malls, up-market hotels and some bars have WiFi internet access.

TOILETS

● Public toilets *(banheiro, lavabo, retretes, WC)* are few and far between; the most hygienic are in restaurants, museums and shopping malls. Bars and cafés also have toilets (hygiene levels may vary); leave a small tip if you are just using the loo.

TOURIST OFFICES

● There are 21 tourist information offices in the Algarve. They have local information and maps.

TAKING PRECAUTIONS

The Algarve is a safe region in a country with low levels of crime, particularly against visitors. Follow common-sense rules, such as carrying little cash and leaving valuable jewellery at home. Don't leave expensive items on view in your car. If you are unfortunate enough to be a victim of crime, you must report your loss to the police and be issued with a crime report in order to claim on your insurance.

CHILDREN

Children are welcomed with open arms by the Portuguese, who will pick up your baby and talk to and fuss over your children. Despite this, there are few facilities for children in the way of changing rooms, special menus, high chairs etc. Hotels will put an extra bed in your room for your child, but they do not have baby-sitting services as children stay up late and go out with their parents. Baby supplies are available in supermarkets everywhere. Watch the strength of the sun; keep children in the shade during the hottest hours (12–4) and slap on a high-factor sun cream at all times. Remember also to keep children well hydrated with regular drinks of water.

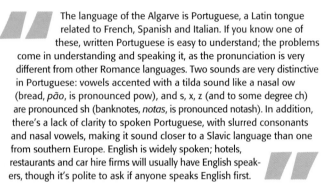

Language

The language of the Algarve is Portuguese, a Latin tongue related to French, Spanish and Italian. If you know one of these, written Portuguese is easy to understand; the problems come in understanding and speaking it, as the pronunciation is very different from other Romance languages. Two sounds are very distinctive in Portuguese: vowels accented with a tilda sound like a nasal ow (bread, *pão*, is pronounced pow), and s, x, z (and to some degree ch) are pronounced sh (banknotes, *notas*, is pronounced notash). In addition, there's a lack of clarity to spoken Portuguese, with slurred consonants and nasal vowels, making it sound closer to a Slavic language than one from southern Europe. English is widely spoken; hotels, restaurants and car hire firms will usually have English speakers, though it's polite to ask if anyone speaks English first.

USEFUL WORDS AND PHRASES

yes	*sim*
no	*não*
good morning	*bom dia*
good afternoon/evening	*boa tarde*
goodnight	*boa noite*
please	*por favor, se faz favor*
thank you	*obrigado/a*
where	*onda*
what	*que*
when	*quando*
why	*porquê*
how	*como*
how much	*quanto*
do you speak English?	*fala ingles?*
I don't know	*nâo sei*
sorry/excuse me	*desculpe*
do you know?	*sabe?*
can you?	*pode?*
now/later	*agora/mais tarde*
more/less	*mais/menos*
big/small	*grande/pequeno*
open/closed	*aberto/fechado*
men/women	*senhoras/homens*
tourist office	*turismo*
beach	*praia*
square	*praça*
church	*igreja*
market	*mercado*
danger	*perigro*

NUMBERS

1	um
2	dois
3	três
4	quatro
5	cinco
6	seis
7	sete
8	oito
9	nove
10	dez
11	onze
12	doze
13	treze
14	catorze
15	quinze
16	dezasseis
17	dezassete
18	dezoito
19	dezanove
20	vinte
30	trinta
40	quarenta
50	cinquenta
60	sessenta
70	setenta
80	oitenta
90	noventa
100	cem
1,000	mil

FOOD AND DRINK	
bread	*pão*
butter	*manteiga*
salt/pepper	*sal/pimenta*
sugar	*açúcar*
olive oil	*azeite*
meat	*carne*
beef	*carne de vaca, bife (steak)*
cured dried ham	*presunto*
lamb	*cordeiro*
pork	*porco*
chicken	*frango*
fish	*peixe*
shellfish	*mariscos*
sardines	*sardinhas*
bream	*dourada*
dried salt cod	*bacalhau*
red mullet	*salmoneta*
sole	*linguada*
shrimps/prawns	*camarãos/gambas*
lobster	*lagosta*
squid	*lulas*
scallops	*vieira*
vegetables	*legumes*
salad	*salada*
chips	*batatas fritas*
rice	*arroz*
puddings/sweets	*doces/pastéis*
ice-cream	*gelado*
custard tarts	*pastéis de nata*
cakes	*bolos*
cheese	*quiejo*
drinks	*bebidas*
water	*água*
mineral water with/	*água mineral com/*
without gas	*sem gas*
beer	*cerveja*
wine (white/red)	*vinho (branco/tinto)*
port	*vinho do Porto*
espresso coffee	*bica*
coffee/milky coffee	*café/galão*
tea	*chá*
fruit juice	*sumo de fruta*

RESTAURANTS	
fish restaurant	*marisqueria*
grill restaurant	*churrasqueria*
patisserie	*pastelaria*
breakfast	*pequeno almoço*
lunch	*almoço*
dinner	*jantar*
table	*mesa*
starter	*entrada*
main course	*prato principal*
pudding	*sobremesa*
bill	*conta*
knife	*faca*
fork	*garfo*
spoon	*colher*
glass	*copo*
menu	*ementa*
bottle	*garrafa*

TRANSPORTATION	
airport	*aeroporto*
bus	*autocarro*
bus station	*estação de autocarro*
bus stop	*paragem*
a ticket to	*um bilhete para*
single	*ida*
return	*ida e volta*
which way to?	*como se vai para?*
how far?	*a que distância?*
where is?	*onde está*
car	*carro*
petrol	*gasolina*
petrol station	*posta de gasolina*

Timeline

LEARNING FROM SPAIN

Developing later as a tourist destination than the Spanish Costas, the Algarve learnt from Spanish mistakes; high-rise buildings and unchecked, sprawling development is limited to a relatively small area, and Faro has retained its low-key charm as the regional capital.

From left: The Forte da Ponte da Bandeira, Lagos; a bronze statue of a knight at Silves Castle; section of the castle walls, Silves; a statue of Henry the Navigator at Lagos; tanks on the streets during the Portuguese revolution in 1974

500BC Greeks and Carthaginians, from modern Tunis, establish Portimão.

197BC Romans invade the Iberian peninsula and settle in the Algarve; all regional resistance quelled by Caesar in 61–45BC.

585 Christian Visigoths take over Iberia; bishopric established at Silves.

711 Moors invade Iberia and penetrate Algarve; by 9th century kingdom of Al-Gharb established with capital at Shelb (Silves).

1189 Silves surrenders to Christian army during Reconquista.

1249 Struggles against the Moors culminate with their expulsion from Tavira and Faro.

1420–1443 Henry the Navigator is based at Sagres, where he brings together a group which lays the foundations for Portugal's pre-eminence as a maritime trading nation.

1444 Slave market established at Lagos, one of the first in Europe.

1580 The Algarve comes under Spanish rule after Philip II conquers Portugal.

1587 Sir Francis Drake sacks Lagos and Sagres.

1668 Spain recognizes Portuguese independence.

1755 The Great Earthquake flattens Lisbon and destroys many towns in the Algarve.

1807 Napoleon invades Portugal; the French are finally expelled in 1811.

1889 Lisbon–Faro railway opens; fish canning and cork industries continue to develop in the Algarve.

1910 Portuguese Republic established.

1932–1968 António de Oliveira Salazar establishes a military dictatorship and rules Portugal.

1965 Faro airport built.

1974 The Carnation Revolution on 25 April; Portugal becomes a democracy.

1986 Portugal joins the EU.

1990–2008 Ongoing tourist development. New east-west motorway built and bridge over River Guadiana to Spain built.

2002 Euro introduced.

2004 Parque de Cidades built near Loulé as Portugal hosts European Football Championship.

2009 Increasing grass-roots concern over excessive water use for golf course irrigation and tourist facilities.

SALAZAR

Dr. Salazar's background was in economics and he came to power to balance Portugal's books, moving from finance minister, to prime minister, to dictator. He succeeded, but at huge cost, stifling Portugal's political, economic and cultural life for almost 40 years, and leaving Portugal the poorest, most backward country in western Europe.

HENRY THE NAVIGATOR

Son of Joaõ I and Philippa of Lancaster, Henry the Navigator (1394–1460) was the impetus behind the opening up of the sea routes to India by the Portuguese. He concentrated on navigation and the development of faster ships and better navigational instruments. He did this at Sagres, gathering a formidable team of specialists around him and had the satisfaction of seeing the Portuguese push further and further south and east. He died in Sagres.

Index

TWINPACK
Algarve

WRITTEN BY Sally Roy
VERIFIED BY Lindsay Bennett and Penny Phenix
COVER DESIGN AND DESIGN WORK Jacqueline Bailey
INDEXER Marie Lorimer
IMAGE RETOUCHING AND REPRO Sarah Montgomery, Michael Moody and James Tims
PROJECT EDITOR Cathy Harrison
SERIES EDITOR Cathy Harrison

© **AA MEDIA LIMITED 2010**
Reprinted April and December 2010

Colour separation by AA Digital Department
Printed and bound by Leo Paper Products, China

A CIP catalogue record for this book is available from the British Library.

ISBN 978-0-7495-6146-8

Published by AA Publishing, a trading name of AA Media Limited, whose registered office is Fanum House, Basing View, Basingstoke, Hampshire RG21 4EA. Registered number 06112600.

Front cover image: AA/M Chaplow
Back cover images: (i) AA/M Chaplow; (ii) AA/C Sawyer; (iii) AA/C Jones; (iv) AA/M Chaplow

A04619
Maps in this title produced from mapping © MAIRDUMONT / Falk Verlag 2011

The Automobile Association would like to thank the following photographers, companies and picture libraries for their assistance in the preparation of this book.

Abbreviations for the pictures credits are as follows – (t) top; (b) bottom; (c) centre; (l) left; (r) right; (AA) AA World Travel Library.

1 AA/M Chaplow; **2–18 top panel** AA/A Kouprianoff; 4 AA/M Chaplow; 5 AA/ A Mockford & N Bonetti; **6tl** AA/C Jones; **6tcl** AA/C Jones; **6tcr** AA/C Jones; **6tr** AA/ C Jones; **6bl** AA/A Kouprianoff; **6bc** AA/C Jones; **6br** AA/C Jones; **7tl** AA/C Jones; **7tc** AA/C Jones; **7tr** AA/C Jones; **7bl** AA/C Jones; **7bc** AA/A Mockford & N Bonetti; **7br** AA/M Chaplow; **10t** AA/C Jones; **10tc** AA/C Jones; **10bc** AA/C Sawyer; **10b** AA/C Jones; **11t** AA/C Jones; **11tc** AA/C Jones; **11bc** AA/A Mockford & N Bonetti; **11b** AA/M Birkitt; **12t** AA/J Edmanson; **12tc** AA/M Chaplow; **12bc** AA/J Edmanson; **12bc** AA/C Jones; **13t** Digitalvision; **13tc** Photodisc; **13b** AA/C Jones; **14t** AA/ C Jones; **14tc** AA/A Kouprianoff; **14bc** AA/C Jones; **14b** AA/M Chaplow; **15** AA/ C Jones; **16t** AA/C Jones; **16tc** AA/C Jones; **16bc** AA/M Birkitt; **16b** AA/J Edmanson; **17t** Brand X Pics; **17tc** AA/C Jones; **17bc** AA/M Chaplow; **17b** Photodisc; **18t** AA/C Jones; **18tc** AA/M Chaplow; **18bc** AA/C Jones; **18b** AA/C Jones; **19t** AA/ A Mockford & N Bonetti; **19tc** AA/M Chaplow; **19bc** AA/C Jones; **19b** AA/ J Edmanson; **20–21** AA/A Mockford & N Bonetti; **24l** AA/M Chaplow; **24r** AA/ M Chaplow; **25** AA/C Jones; **26l** AA/C Jones; **26/27ct** AA/A Kouprianoff; **26/27cb** AA/C Jones; **27r** AA/C Jones; **28** AA/A Mockford & N Bonetti; **28/29** AA/A Mockford & N Bonetti; **29** AA/A Mockford & N Bonetti; **30** AA/C Jones; **31** AA/A Kouprianoff; **32l** AA/A Mockford & N Bonetti; **32/33t** AA/A Mockford & N Bonetti; **32/33b** AA/A Mockford & N Bonetti; **33r** AA/C Jones; **34** AA/A Mockford & N Bonetti; **35t** AA/A Mockford & N Bonetti; **35bl** AA/M Chaplow; **35br** AA/C Jones; **36** AA/C Jones; **37** AA/ M Chaplow; **38** AA/J Edmanson; **39** AA/A Mockford & N Bonetti; **40** AA/ J Edmanson; **41** AA/C Jones; **42** AA/M Chaplow; **43–44** AA/C Sawyer; **45** AA/ J Edmanson; **46l** AA/M Chaplow; **46tr** AA/M Chaplow; **46br** AA/M Chaplow; **47t** AA/A Kouprianoff; **47bl** AA/M Chaplow; **47br** AA/J Edmanson; **48t** AA/C Jones; **48bl** AA/C Jones; **48br** AA/C Jones; **49t** AA/C Jones; **49bl** AA/C Jones; **49br** AA/ C Jones; **52l** AA/C Jones; **52ct** AA/C Jones; **52cb** AA/C Jones; **53t** AA/C Jones; **53bl** AA/A Kouprianoff; **53br** AA/C Jones; **54** AA/M Birkitt; **55t** AA/C Jones; **55bl** AA/C Jones; **55br** AA/C Jones; **56l** AA/M Chaplow; **56tl** AA/M Birkitt; **56bl** AA/ A Kouprianoff; **57t** AA/J Edmanson; **57bl** AA/M Chaplow; **57br** AA/M Chaplow; **58** AA/C Jones; **59/60t** AA/C Jones; **59bl** AA/C Jones; **59br** AA/C Jones; **60l** AA/M Chaplow; **60r** AA/C Jones; **61t** AA/M Chaplow; **62** AA/M Birkitt; **63** AA/ J Edmanson; **64–65t** AA/C Jones; **65b–66** AA/C Sawyer; **67** AA/J Edmanson; **70l** AA/C Jones; **70r** AA/C Jones; **71t** AA/M Birkitt; **71l** AA/C Jones; **71r** AA/C Jones; **72l** AA/M Chaplow; **72c** AA/M Chaplow; **72r** AA/M Chaplow; **73l** AA/M Chaplow; **73r** AA/M Birkitt; **74** AA/C Jones; **74/75** AA/C Jones; **75** AA/C Jones; **76** AA/C Jones; **77t** AA/C Jones; **77bl** AA/M Chaplow; **77br** AA/C Jones; **78/79t** AA/M Chaplow; **78l** AA/C Jones; **78/79r** AA/M Chaplow; **79r** AA/M Chaplow; **80l** AA/M Chaplow; **80r** Jose Manuel; **81l** AA/C Jones; **81r** AA/C Jones; **82/83t** AA/J Edmanson; **82l** AA/ A Mockford & N Bonetti; **82r** AA/M Chaplow; **83l** AA/M Chaplow; **83r** AA/C Jones; **84** AA/C Jones; **85** AA/J Edmanson; **86** AA/C Jones; **87–88** AA/C Sawyer; **89** AA/ M Chaplow; **92l** AA/C Jones; **92r** AA/J Edmanson; **93** AA/C Jones; **94** AA/ M Chaplow; **95t** AA/M Chaplow; **95bl** AA/A Mockford & N Bonetti; **95br** Courtesy of the Algarve Promotion Bureau; **96** AA/M Chaplow; **97** AA/M Chaplow; **98t** AA/ C Jones; **98bl** AA/M Chaplow; **98br** AA/C Jones; **99l** AA/C Jones; **99tr** AA/C Jones; **99br** AA/C Jones; **100t** AA/A Kouprianoff; **100bl** AA/J Edmanson; **100br** AA/ A Kouprianoff; **101** AA/M Birkitt; **102t** AA/M Chaplow; **102bl** AA/M Chaplow; **102br** AA/M Chaplow; **103** AA/M Chaplow; **104** AA/J Edmanson; **105** AA/C Jones; **106** AA/C Sawyer; **107** AA/A Mockford & N Bonetti; **108–112 top panel** AA/C Sawyer; **108t(i)** Royalty Free Photodisc; **108ct(II)** AA/P Wilson; **108cb(iii)** Stockbyte Royalty Free; **108b (iv)** AA/C Jones; **113** AA/C Jones; **114–125 top panel** AA/ A Kouprianoff; **117** AA/C Sawyer; **119** AA/C Sawyer; **124l** AA/C Jones; **124c** AA/ M Birkitt; **124/125** AA/M Birkitt; **125c** AA/C Jones; **125r** Keystone/Getty Images.

Every effort has been made to trace the copyright holders, and we apologise in advance for any accidental errors. We would be happy to apply any corrections in the following edition of this publication.